Life's Short,

Talk Fast

Life's Short,
Talk Fast

Fifteen Writers
on Why We Can't Stop
Watching *Gilmore Girls*

Edited by Ann Hood

W. W. NORTON & COMPANY

Independent Publishers Since 1923

For my Rory

Contents

Introduction

Ann Hood

Are you #TeamLogan or #TeamJess?

If you don't know what that means, you have somehow missed the phenomenon that is *Gilmore Girls*. But here you are, holding a book, *this* book, *Life's Short, Talk Fast: Fifteen Writers on Why We Can't Stop Watching* Gilmore Girls. Welcome to the world of Stars Hollow and its lovable, irritating, funny, warm-hearted, smart, fast-talking citizens. Welcome to the world of *Gilmore Girls*.

Gilmore Girls, created by Amy Sherman-Palladino, is the television show that debuted in 2000, ran for seven seasons, and has been in syndication for almost twenty years. It has bonded real-life mothers and daughters together since the iconic pilot introduced us to Lorelai and Rory Gilmore and their idyllic Connecticut town of Stars Hollow.

Lorelai is the fast-talking, coffee-drinking, miniskirted mom who had Rory when she was just sixteen years old. Rory, sixteen when the show begins, is an overachiever who has her sights set on Harvard. Their hometown of Stars Hollow is populated with an endearing cast of characters: Sally Struthers as the duo's wacky neighbor; Sookie—Melissa McCarthy's first role—the chirpy friend and chef; Broadway star Kelly Bishop as Lorelai's judgmental mom; Edward Herrmann as the bumbling dad. Carole King is the record store owner. Norman Mailer eats at the local inn.

Although the plot is mostly driven by wondering if Lorelai will end up with Christopher (Rory's father), Luke (the local diner owner who has loved her since episode 1), or one of the suitors who appear from season to season, the real story is mother-daughter relationships. Lorelai's fractured one with her own mother; Rory and Lorelai's developing one as Rory moves from private high school to college to life as a journalist.

I know this anthology of writers writing about *Gilmore Girls* will appeal to the legions of fans who, according to the *New York Times*, are still feverish about the show and its characters. "Few would have predicted in 2000 that the show still endures all these years later," the *NYT* says. But not only does the show get rewatched by its diehard fans, it also gains new fans every year, partially due to its easy availability on Netflix and partially because its themes and characters are still relevant and appeal to mothers and daughters today. Sheila Lawrence, a longtime writer for the show, says that fans fall into two categories: "Either they have a Lorelai-and-Rory relationship, or they desperately wish they had a Lorelai-and-Rory relationship."

Mothers and daughters don't just watch *Gilmore Girls*, they watch it over and over, reciting iconic lines along with Rory and Lorelai, crying when Rory and Lorelai fight, crying when their love is so real that it's like they are telling *your* story.

The week before my daughter left for college, we watched our favorite episodes every night. We didn't even have to confirm which we'd watch because our favorites are stamped in our joint consciousness. The pilot, of course. "Scene in a Mall." "The Deer Hunters." "Take the Deviled Eggs." "The Lorelais' First Day at Yale" . . . I sent her off to college with a Chilton Academy T-shirt (Rory's alma mater); she called the first week to tell me she'd had a Marty experience—if you're a fan, you know what that means.

The one thing my daughter and I disagree about is that she is #TeamJess and I am #TeamLogan, which I explore in my essay "In Omnia Paratus." Joanna Rakoff, Katie Moulton, Yassmin Abdel-Magied, and Anjanette Delgado explore motherhood and daughterhood—their own and Lorelai's, Rory's, and Emily's. Nina de Gramont and Erin Almond explore class, one through Lorelai's many coats, the other through a very different view of Connecticut. Freya North tells us about the joys of watching *Gilmore Girls* with her son. Sanjena Sathian's essay "Hiding in the Floorboards," originally published in *Vox*, explores the character of Lane Kim, who is from a conservative immigrant family similar to her own. Cathi Hanauer, forbidden to watch anything except *Masterpiece Theatre* growing up, wonders if *Gilmore Girls* can make her, finally, normal. Tracey Minkin, a bookworm herself, writes about Rory's bookishness. And Annabelle Mei defends Rory's choices that turned one of television's most loved characters into one of its most hated.

You will find essays by men here too. Francesco Sedita watched the show during the pandemic and discovered its themes of what makes a home. Rand Richards Cooper resisted its charms when his wife and teenager watched, but slowly started warming to the show when his brother-in-law—a *Gilmore Girls* fan—became ill. Michael Ruhlman, my own darling husband, learned that the charms of the show might help him forge new relationships. And being friends with Chris Eigemen, a.k.a. Jason "Digger" Stiles, didn't hurt either.

But oy with the poodles already! Grab a cup of coffee and prepare to be Gilmored.

Life's Short,

Talk Fast

In Omnia Paratus

Ann Hood

In the summer of 1973, all I wanted to do was kiss boys. Cute boys, to be exact. Best of all: cute boys with sexy cars—Mustang convertibles, flirty MGs, souped-up Camaros. I was sixteen years old and worked as a department store model at the Warwick Mall and that summer boys were everywhere. There were the Jordan Marsh stock boys, their muscles bulging beneath white T-shirts as they wheeled racks of men's suits or wedding gowns through the store; there was the green-eyed boy who worked in the bookstore; the curly-haired boy who worked in the record store; the college boys in their summer jobs at the mall.

I was a good girl, meaning that all I did was kiss the boys. Not even second base as our bodies pressed together, the stick shift between us, the boy groaning with pleasure and frustration, his hand creeping up my shirt and down my cutoff jeans, me slapping it away. Such power I had that summer! And although I was a good girl, I was not a very nice one. One night, a college boy working in the shoe department took me to dinner at Valle's Steak House. He picked me up in his father's very unsexy Ford and wore a very unsexy brown suit. By the time I was cutting into my filet mignon, I was finished with him. My mind wandered. He ordered a second martini, I thought about the book waiting for me at home. I thought about the cute boy who was taking me to the movies the next night. I could see his heart breaking all the way through to the cheesecake, but I didn't care.

Now, fifty years later, I care. The adult me worries constantly about hurting people's feelings. I help people who are lost in my Greenwich Village neighborhood and make dinner for my students. I listen to my friends' problems, even when deadlines are pounding on my door. But that sixteen-year-old me did not think twice about a teenage boy's tender heart. I was tall and blond and tanned from spending long days on the beach slathered in Coppertone and eating root beer Popsicles, talking about boys with my friend Beth. My power felt so enormous that my nerves actually tingled with it. I walked around with an electric current shooting through my body, and that electricity drew boys to me.

One of those boys was a kid from school named Roland. He was skinny and he needed braces and he had acne. Maybe worst of all, Roland rode his bike everywhere. I would have ignored him completely, but he was my good friend, one of the small clique of smart kids who hung around together in a school where being smart was only considered an asset by the teachers. Roland and I laughed our way through chemistry class and sold candy bars in the cafeteria to raise money for the school. We often did group projects with our friends to ensure getting an A and ate pizza or doughnuts while we worked diligently at someone's kitchen table.

That summer of 1973, Roland rode his bike to my house a lot. I'd come home from the beach, sand clinging to my suntan lotion, hair wet, and my mother would tell me that Roland had come by. Again. "Just tell that poor boy you're not interested," she said. "We're just *friends*," I snapped. I'd come home from work only to find out that Roland had stopped by again. He always had iced tea with my mother when I wasn't there, which made me mad at both of them. That he had pedaled his bike four and a half miles in ninety-degree weather to "stop by" never occurred to me.

If I was home when he showed up, we sat on the back porch and talked about our summers. I see now that Roland actually did interesting things, like climbing Mount Washington and biking around Cape Cod, while all I did was stand in the Jordan Marsh window in autumn "school clothes" mannequin modeling, which meant not moving except once every two hours, lie on the beach with Beth, and kiss boys. But back then, Roland seemed about as uncool as a person could be. Why would someone hike over six thousand feet just for a view? Why bike around Cape Cod when you could drive? But since we were *only friends*, I listened and teased him that he was too pale and needed to go to the beach more.

Then, one day, driving down Route 2 on my way home from the beach, I saw the sign at the Warwick Musical Theatre announcing its upcoming shows. Engelbert Humperdinck, Tom Jones, Liberace, and then, coming on July 21 for one night only: George Carlin. Anyone who came of age in the 1960s and '70s adored George Carlin, could recite his Seven Words You Can Never Say on Television perfectly and quote the weather report he gave as the Hippy-Dippy Weatherman: "Weather tonight: dark. Turning partly light by morning." George Carlin was one of the few cultural touchpoints I shared with my five-years-older-than-me brother and my younger cousins. *Everyone* loved George Carlin.

From the minute I saw that sign, I made it a mission to get a cute boy with a sexy car to take me to the show. The red-haired boy who went to the fancy private school. The blond stock boy with eyes like Paul McCartney. The bookstore boy, the record store boy, the new boy who worked at Jordan Marsh in the linens department. I let them all know that I wanted to see George Carlin more than anything. Then the phone calls came, all with the same bad news: The show is completely sold out. I had my eyes set that week on the blond stock boy, so to him I persisted. "There has to be two tickets somewhere . . ." I complained to Roland one afternoon as he sat, sweaty from the long bike ride, guzzling lemonade. "Completely sold out? There are over three thousand seats! How can it be sold out?"

And then, just days before the concert, a miracle. I was at home, sitting in front of the box fan in the living room, when the phone rang.

"I got two tickets!" a boy said. "To George Carlin!"

My excitement would have been even bigger if the boy had been anyone but Roland. But Roland it was, the procurer of the sought-after tickets.

"You want to go, right?" he said.

"Yes!" I did want to go, and if seeing George Carlin live and in person meant going with my pal, then so be it.

In my memory, the phone rang again minutes later, though it might have been the next night.

"I got two tickets!" a boy said. "To George Carlin!"

Not just *a* boy. *The* boy. The blond stock boy with Paul McCartney eyes.

"You want to go, right?" he said.

"Yes!"

"With me?" he said.

"Yes!"

Great, he would pick me up at six on Saturday night.

Lost in the joy of a date with the blond stock boy, it took a few minutes for my predicament to become clear to me.

My mother was sitting at the kitchen table, drinking black coffee and smoking Pall Malls, a game of solitaire spread out before her.

"Mom, you have to do me a favor," I said.

She narrowed her eyes behind her bifocals. "What would

that be?" she asked, cigarette between her lips, a four of hearts suspended in the air. My mother and I always got along just fine, but this summer I was pushing her patience. A lot.

"You have to call Roland and tell him I can't go to George Carlin with him Saturday night."

"Why can't you go? All I've been hearing about for weeks is George Carlin."

"Because that cute stock boy asked me to go!" I said, exasperated.

Mom put down her cigarette. "Do you honestly believe I'm going to call that poor kid and break his heart for you?"

"Yes!"

She leveled a cold gaze at me. "Ann," she said, "I know you and I know that you will do the right thing in this situation."

I stared back at her. She resumed her game of solitaire.

"Fine," I said, and stomped into the living room, where I called Roland and told him that I had to work on Saturday night.

Oh! The blond stock boy picked me up in his Pontiac Trans Am, muscles bulging beneath his baby blue shirt, hair curling just right over his collar. It was July in Rhode Island, hot and sticky and full of promise. He held my hand as we made our way through the crowd, showed our tickets to the usher, and led me into our row. Right beside Roland and his brother.

Roland looked at me and then he looked at the stock boy and he sunk deep into his seat. I do not remember if George Carlin said the seven dirty words or played the Hippy-Dippy Weatherman. I only remember wanting to disappear, to run out into that summer night and just keep running, maybe forever.

It comes as no surprise that Roland never spoke to me again, not even at our twenty-fifth high school reunion. He went away to college and became a doctor, whereas the stock boy still lives in his little hometown, where he has grown round and stagnant. I spotted him not long ago, sitting in a plastic-webbed lawn chair drinking a beer in front of the fire station.

By the time that summer ended, I'd had my heart broken by a college boy named Peter who worked in men's wear. For the whole month of August, we went to the beach on our days off and made out in his charmille green Citroën. We ate cheese-burgers and ice cream sundaes, frozen lemonade and A&W root beer. He made me so dizzy I couldn't even concentrate on *Camelot*, which was rereleased at the movies that summer, and struggled to discuss Guinevere's fate with him afterward. But then Labor Day came and he went back to college and never called me again.

What does any of this—Roland, the stock boy, Peter and his Citroën—have to do with the television show *Gilmore Girls* or Logan Huntzberger and Rory Gilmore?

Well, everything.

After my second divorce (a story for another essay), I was about as crushed as a person can be. Twenty-five years, three children—and the loss of our second child, Grace, when she was just five—a home built in 1792 that I tended and nurtured, all came crashing down in the ugliest ways possible (this, too, is for another essay). I was broke and broken. And forced to leave that sweet home of mine because I didn't have the money to buy out my ex. At almost sixty years old, I had to borrow money from my mother and have her cosign the mortgage on a new home, which added to my enormous sense of failure.

My preteen daughter and I moved into a loft in a renovated factory across town, in a neighborhood that was far from gentrified. But it had enormous windows, loads of sunlight, high ceilings, and a modern kitchen. In other words, it was the complete opposite of the home I'd left. Our first night there, we ate spaghetti carbonara, our plates balanced on unpacked boxes because we had no dining room table.

As mothers do, or try to do, I pointed out all of the wonderful new things in our lives. The high school she wanted to go to was literally next door! Our new neighbors were great! We were getting two kittens!

Gently, my daughter said, "I know just the thing we need." She picked up the two television remotes that I had not yet figured out how to use, pressed some buttons, and continued, "It's this show that I think we are going to love. I've only seen the first couple of episodes . . ."

And just like that, the TV screen filled with the faces of Lorelai and Rory Gilmore. When the opening song, "Where You Lead (I Will Follow)," played, we found ourselves singing along enthusiastically, pointing to each other and high-fiving, laughing and crying in our new home.

Every night, we ate our dinner on unpacked boxes and watched *Gilmore Girls*, each time belting out "Where You Lead (I Will Follow)" with Carole King. Some nights we only watched two episodes; sometimes we watched as many as five. Luckily for us, there are 153 episodes, enough to finally unpack all those boxes, get a dining room table, and start high school. We watched Rory fall in love with Dean in high school, break up with him to go out with Jess, break up with Jess and go back with Dean, and meet Logan Huntzberger in college at Yale.

Every *Gilmore Girls* fan is on a team—either Team Dean, Team Jess, or Team Logan. To me, Dean was the perfect high school boyfriend: adorable, sweet, adoring, and a little jealous. Jess, Luke's nephew who sweeps into town and turns everything upside down—including Rory—is that bad boy with a hot temper. He likes to kiss and scowl and pick fights. But Logan. Logan! Handsome. Rich. Smart. He offered Rory so much—exciting adventures, a new way of life, the opportunity to step away from everything she knew and see a different world.

When cub reporter Rory starts investigating the Life and Death Brigade, a secret society at Yale, Logan invites her to one of its events—glamping in the woods. The highlight of the weekend is dressing up in formal attire and jumping off a seven-foot platform while holding an umbrella. At first good girl Rory refuses, but Logan convinces her to do "something stupid, something bad for you." And so she jumps. The Life and Death's motto is, after all, In Omnia Paratus. Ready for anything.

"I hate him," my daughter announced when Rory and Logan stole a boat in season 5, episode 21, "Blame Booze and Melville."

"You hate Logan?" I asked, stunned.

"He just got her arrested!"

"No, no. She's the one who wanted to steal the boat. He said, 'It's not ours to take.' And she said, 'Let's go.'"

"They end up in jail!"

We stared at each other, each of us thinking, *Who is this person?*

"I hope we can both agree Dean is not right for her," I finally said as a peace offering.

"Obviously."

In college, I fell for one wrong guy after another, always because they were so damn cute. The one who looked like John Denver, so sweet and enamored of me? No interest. The one in my Shakespeare class who always walked with me out of Independence Hall, asking me what I thought of *Hamlet*, of *Lear*, of *The Merchant of Venice*? I talked animatedly until we hit the quad, then I focused on finding the darling, aloof boy who drove a 1950s Cadillac so he could break my heart. By college, I had somehow stopped being the heartbreaker and become the wounded one, so that after I graduated, I protected my heart, dating randomly and without enthusiasm.

It is fair to say that I dated my share of Deans—nice, dull guys who liked me too much—but mostly I dated Logans, those devilish men who took me for lavish dinners and smiled their beautiful smiles, who fell in love with me but couldn't commit. My daughter was right, why did I think Logan was so perfect, not just for Rory but in general? Why was I still so won over by cute guys who drove nice cars? Hadn't my ex-husband been that very type, rolling into my life in a vintage Mercedes with a dazzling grin?

At every opportunity I reminded my daughter about Jess's flaws. How he lied to Luke about skipping school. How he lied about being in a fight with Dean. How he cruelly made out with someone else right in front of Rory. How he kisses Rory when she's still going out with Dean.

But then, in season 6, episode 8, after Rory has dropped out of Yale, when she is living with her grandmother and still dating partying, drinking Logan, Jess shows up out of the blue and gives her a copy of the novel he has just published. They go out for a celebratory dinner, only to have Logan show up and act like a horse's ass, putting down Jess and blabbering about himself. As we watch, flashes of so many dinner dates with so many boys crossed my mind, the fake smiles as I listened to them talk about their hockey games, their sailboats, God help me, their insurance business.

"This isn't you," Jess tells Rory when he walks out of the restaurant. "I *know* you."

And then, just like in *Gilmore Girls*, I met my Jess. A writer who has sowed his oats, who loves me truly, who is cuter than Logan Huntzberger or any of those guys in my past. But unlike Rory, and thanks to my personal Rory, I don't let him go. I keep him.

But I am still steadfastly Team Logan. I know that of course Jess is the right one for Rory, but I also know that Rory, and my daughter, and I, all of us need a Logan. We need to have our hearts broken, and to break hearts. We need to cry on our friend's shoulder while we eat leftover Chinese food, and we need to sit, hot and uncomfortable, beside someone who loves us that we do not love. We need to jump into the unknown and then pull ourselves up, bruised and aching, and jump again.

Daughter: Be kinder than I was, but don't hold on to something that was never maybe yours in the first place. Outgrow your Logans, hopefully faster than I did. And then one day you will be in Vermont on a sunny August afternoon, or in a crowded lecture hall with an autumn wind banging the windows, or sipping a bourbon at a zinc bar, and your Jess, the person who *knows* you, will call out to you. And if you are ready, you will hear him. In Omnia Paratus.

Mom, Please

Joanna Rakoff

Two-plus decades ago, on a blistering December evening, I turned on the television—for the first time in perhaps a year—and found something I'd never encountered before: Two women talking. Two dark-haired women talking. And talking and talking. Their conversation went on far past the point of comfort, much like my own conversations with friends, bearing the weight of each other's deepest thoughts and fears; much, too, like the conversations in the screwball comedies I'd watched as a kid with my Greatest Generation dad, a former borscht belt comedian for whom banter represented both the highest form of art and the purest expression of love. Clearly, the two brunettes on the screen in front of me felt the same.

At first, the relationship between these two women—who

were beautiful, but in an unvarnished, vulnerable way I'd, again, never encountered on the small screen—baffled me. Were they sisters, with a large gap between them, like my own sister and myself? Or aunt and niece? Friends? But as I watched that first episode—in which Rory attends a dance at her new school, a book (of course) in her bag, to disastrous end—it became clear that they were mother and daughter, joking with and prodding each other, while holding each other to a high level of honesty, emotional and otherwise.

Mother and daughter. Those words meant something very different to me than the relationship I watched unfold over the course of that bleak winter and spring. Because, you see, my own mother bore a remarkable, almost uncanny resemblance to Emily Gilmore, in every possible way. So much so that certain lines and scenes felt akin to watching a home movie. My mother, Phyllis, had Emily's dark, enormous, deep-set eyes and impossibly high cheekbones, her dancer's posture and commanding presence, her style of speech and helmet of hair, her love of department stores. Emily's pleated trousers and tailored blouses and St. John suits and court shoes could have arrived on set directly from my mother's closets. She, too, could not keep a maid—though she called them "housekeepers"—and felt entirely comfortable ordering around every human in her presence. (Every time Emily commanded a uniformed servant to "bring this to the dining room" or directed Lorelai to "sit down," I gave a little shudder.)

But mostly, or most importantly, Phyllis and Emily shared a sharply defined set of values and expectations for their

Mom, Please   15

children—for, I suppose, the children of everyone in their milieu—and a coolly rigid idea of what constitutes acceptable behavior, dress, grooming, interests, activities, and goals. Not to mention meals, travel destinations, and styles. (Once, as a small child, I suggested to my mother that we go camping. "Animals sleep outside," she told me. "People sleep in hotels." Hotels only. Motels never.) Acceptable sports: tennis and golf. Acceptable dinner conversation: school, work, gossip of a non-tawdry nature, travel plans. Acceptable fabrics for bodily adornment: cashmere, wool, silk, linen, cotton. Acceptable daytime shoes for women: loafers or pumps with a one- or two-inch heel, composed of leather or suede, inside and out. "Anything higher is an evening shoe." In my mother's coda—about which I could fill an entire book—sneakers were only acceptable when engaging in a sport, miniskirts were only acceptable before the age of thirty (as was hair below the shoulders), and meals could only be eaten with actual silverware, not "that plastic stuff." In eleventh grade, my mother suggested I drop one of my best friends because she wore a translucent skirt without a slip. A sign, Phyllis explained, of both poor judgment and bad character.

In short, the house, the world, the worldview from which Lorelai sought escape was similar, if not exactly identical, to that which I myself found so frustrating, so stifling, so soulcrushing. This world, centered on an elaborate set of societal rules, allowed no room for any sort of feeling. Midway through that first season, I burst into huge, gulping sobs as Emily sharply tells Lorelai, a vicious edge to her voice, "You always let your emotions get in the way. That's the problem with you, Lorelai. You don't think." This had been my mother's mantra, of sorts, with regard to me, along with "You're so sensitive. You let everything get to you." And I, like Lorelai in that scene, always, always fought tears, knowing they would only make my mother angrier. "Mom, please," she says, gently, begging, with those two words, for her mother to regard her with empathy, to try, just try, to see things from her point of view, or to allow her to have feelings, to fall in love, to be hurt, or disappointed, or sad, or excited; to see, even, that in Lorelai's universe—and in mine—decisions can be made, must be made, based on emotional inclinations rather than societal expectations. I had uttered those exact words, through tears, my voice ragged with pain, to my own mother. Though not for some time. I had—just as Lorelai before the show starts—given up on my mother, given up on the possibility of her regarding me with warmth and understanding, rather than coldness and judgment.

Perhaps now is the moment to explain that though I'm telling you all this now, with the benefit of hindsight, during that first season—perhaps the first three or four or five—the true beating heart of my intense, obsessive love for the show lay in Rory. Because, you see, despite my mother's constant disappointment in me, I myself bore an uncanny resemblance to Rory, rather than Lorelai. And the show, from that first episode, changed my life—this sounds like an exaggeration but I assure you it is not—because I had never, not ever, seen a person so like myself represented on any screen, big or small.

In books, yes—hello, *Anne of Green Gables!*—but television and film seemed reserved for glossier types, even if they owned bookstores or

went to Harvard. Me: a person who carried books in her bag, even to school dances, even (in my case) to her grandmother's funeral. Who preferred sitting on the couch with my best friend to even the most hyped party. Unabashedly ambitious—intellectually, academically, creatively—but incapable of and repulsed by ruthlessness and unkindness. A person for whom getting dressed meant sweaters and army pants, and getting dressed up meant floral dresses that hit below the knee, even as a kid in the era of bandage skirts, an era best exemplified by Sandy's transformation, at the end of *Grease*, from elegant, demure bobby-soxer to big-haired vixen in skintight pants. A person who couldn't stand the idea of hurting anyone or anything. Maybe most importantly: a hopelessly earnest person, who had come of age in an era of irony.

My mother's disappointment in me lay not in my constant and endless rebellion, but in my quiet rejection of her values and expectations, and in my disregard for the material and behavioral minutiae she believed more important than anything, anything at all. My rejection, I suppose, of her particular style of bourgeois. My family, as a whole, was one of merchants and doctors, restaurateurs and engineers. Hardworking people who earned money for solid houses in acceptable suburbs and tennis games on the weekends and spring breaks spent skiing in Park City or Vail. If life derailed them with tragedies—and it had, it certainly had, on both sides, and in my own immediate family—they put it aside, put it to the backs of their organized brains, and showed up to work in the radiology department at Montefiore or the private equity department at Schwab. And I, from childhood, could not put anything to the side. I could not swallow my fears of the dark or the snakes in our backyard or the bullies at school. And as I grew older, I realized that I didn't want to. That I didn't want the life of my parents, my aunts, my cousins. Or that maybe I was constitutionally incapable of it. Just like Lorelai.

Of course, Lorelai left and never looked back, fueled by an unshakable confidence and strength—"You're the most confident person I've ever met," Luke tells her in season 2—by a faith that she could construct a place for herself in the world. Or, really, that if she left Emily's World, she could raise Rory to possess that confidence, no matter what her inclinations, no matter who she turned out to be. A confidence I utterly lacked. Growing up in a version of Emily's World—the New York Jewish version—I spent every minute of every day believing myself to be wrong, wrong, wrong. Wrong for wanting to read all day, for not dropping Debby when she failed to put on a slip, for spending entire days in the nineteenth-century European wing of the Met, a great lump in my throat as I gazed into the complicated faces of Manet's women. Wrong for bursting into tears at a cruel word or for trying to talk to my mother about the cruel word rather than the new fabric she'd chosen for our living room couch.

Until Rory. Who was like me, minus the shame. And minus the loneliness. For she had her mother, always. She had a mother with whom she could talk through everything and anything, without fear of condemnation, without fear of losing her mother's love.

That year—that first-season year—I made some radical changes to my life: I stopped going to dinner parties and party-parties simply because it was expected of me—as a twenty-eight-year-old New Yorker—and I began to consciously consider both my ambition and my storm-like emotions to be assets rather than flaws. And I began to think, too, about what it meant to be a mother. I had been married for two years and had, for those two years, deflected the pressure—from my husband, my parents, the entire fucking world—to have kids, in part because I still felt like a kid myself, still in the thrall of my mother's judgments and expectations, but also in part because I didn't understand how to be a mother unlike my own. But now, suddenly, I saw that a very different style of motherhood was possible, one that made sense to me.

Seven years later, I watched *Gilmore Girls'* final season as my first child slept in his toddler bed four hundred feet away, reading through essays—I held the Rory-like position of features editor at an online magazine—on commercial breaks. So many of my choices, already, had been informed not by parenting books—I'd not even read one—but by Lorelai: To respond with warmth, rather than coldness, even to tantrums. To never question my son's emotions or the way he experienced life. To treat him, always, with the respect I'd accord a dear friend, the respect I wanted. To regard each day as an adventure. To allow him as much independence as I could—an unusual choice in the days of mothers following their kids around playgrounds—and to always keep my sense of humor, even in the hardest moments. Lorelai was my comfort, my motivation, my lodestar.

A year after that final season, my second child, a girl, arrived, and if anything, Lorelai became even more of my model of motherhood, even as it became more difficult to maintain that sense of humor and give both kids the full force of my attention without losing myself, without letting them "run through [me] as a dye runs through water," in the words of Rachel Cusk.

Years passed and they grew into decidedly Rory-like teens: precocious readers and writers, hilarious companions, compassionate friends. And one evening, four-odd years ago—in that first bleak lockdown winter—I had the rare, odd thought that I had succeeded; I had forged a different style of motherhood than the one in which I had been raised, informed by, if not identical to, that of Lorelai. This was followed by a second thought: that my kids—sixteen and twelve—were old enough to watch *Gilmore Girls*.

And so we settled into the big, shabby couch in our small, weird New England house—a house not unlike Lorelai's, with its bedroom off the kitchen and its dated cabinets—and began watching. Rarely, at that time, did the kids agree on anything, but they both immediately began laughing over the parallels between Lorelai and myself. "That's so Mama," they cried as Lorelai begged for coffee and ate fat slices of cake and joked around about literally everything. "Oh my god, Mama, that's literally you," they shouted as she endlessly quoted movies of different eras and dropped her voice two registers in imitation of Dean. And they both fell in love with Rory and the inhabitants of Stars Hollow—Kirk, especially—and argued over Dean versus Jess. And they saw, too, the stark resemblances between Emily and their strong-willed, regal grandmother. "I think Grandma has that exact outfit," Coleman said, over and over. "Didn't Grandma say almost exactly that to you last time we visited?" Pearl asked once, shaking her head in astonishment.

"Yes," I said to both of them, a smile fixed on my face. But in reality, I was fighting tears, a sob lodged uncomfortably in my chest, where it would stay for the weeks—months?—in which we watched all seven seasons. I had watched those seasons how many times—four? five? more?—but this time around—with my giant teens snuggled against me, commenting on every single scene in a Rory-and-Lorelai (and, I suppose, me-and-my-dad) manner—the show hit me differently than it had in years past. For I found myself sympathizing with—okay, identifying with—Emily Gilmore, whom I'd previously viewed as verging on villainous, much as I saw my own chilly, etiquette-ruled mother. Now, she struck me as a tragic figure, a woman who had given her sole daughter everything—every privilege, yes, but also the full force of her energy and love—only to have that daughter run away, completely breaking contact with her parents, at age sixteen.

Coleman was sixteen. A tall, handsome, brilliant boy—six foot three, with a full beard and an elegant, minimalist mode of dress—who, despite his manly aspect, liked to rest his head on my shoulder while we watched. Like Emily, I had poured my everything—my ideas, my values, my passions—into him, into raising him; I had striven to give him everything I lacked as a kid, all the access to worlds intellectual and literary and academic, my full support of his every inclination, the sense that I loved him unconditionally, for his true self, and wanted him only to be that self, nothing else.

As we sat on the sofa, night after night, my mind obsessively turned over the possibility of Coleman absconding in the night, never to be heard from again, of Coleman dropping out of high school and finding work cleaning hotel rooms, of Coleman morphing into a stranger who despised me, rejecting his family, his home, his life. There's a moment in the second season when Rory shows Emily the cottage in which she and Lorelai lived in her earliest years; Emily's face grows slack with sadness and loss, a look I'd seen on my mother's face many times—when she saw my decrepit first apartment in New York, for instance—and one that still held the power to hollow me out with sorrow. A few days later, Emily asks Lorelai, in a hoarse, impassioned voice, "You hated us that much? You had to take that little girl away, that was bad enough, but to live there . . . I saw what you chose over your own family. You would have lived in the gutter, in the street, in a cardboard box, anywhere as long as you didn't have to be near us."

For years, I'd laughed in recognition at Lorelai's disgust with her mother. Now, for the first time, the weight of my own mother's sorrow and loss hit me, with the force of a boulder. She had raised me to be a part of her life, the life she knew and loved, and I had rejected it, wholesale, and made clear my disdain for all she held dear, my disdain for her. What if Coleman walked out of my life and never came back? Or Pearl? It would break me. I knew it would.

Suddenly I saw Emily not as a monster of superficiality, but as a woman eviscerated by the loss of her only child. My mother had lost two children—literally; my older brother and sister were killed in a car accident—and had another, my eldest sister, renounce her and run away, in a manner similar to Lorelai. She, too, I saw now, was less a monster than I'd previously believed, less a monster, more a mother afraid to give herself over to a child—me—who might betray her and all she believed.

Throughout those weeks—months?—I ached to run to my mother, to tell her how sorry I was, how I knew she was doing her best, that she loved me and wanted the best for me, that I knew my life—the choices I'd made, from college to career to shoes—baffled her and hurt her, and I'd never wanted to hurt her.

Except maybe I had.

Maybe, maybe I had. Maybe I wasn't the kind, earnest, empathic girl I'd always believed myself to be. Maybe I didn't care what had happened to my mother in her mysterious childhood—about which I'd been told to never ask her—or the unthinkable losses she'd suffered or the reasons she adhered so rigidly to the coda that governed every choice she made, every day of her life, the coda that maybe kept her sane and functioning, that gave life meaning when it felt like the world was ending.

Maybe I didn't care at all. Maybe all I cared about was myself. Maybe I was still that little girl crying "Mom, please," the smocking on my dress wet with tears, as I tried to tell my mother about the nightmare that had woken me, or the boy who'd ripped open my heart, or the friend who'd betrayed me. My whole life had been a game of Mom, please.

A few months ago, my mother—at ninety-three—wound up in the hospital with viral pneumonia, a potentially deadly illness for someone her age. And indeed, within three days, she was unconscious and her doctor transferred her to a nearby hospice. As I sat by her bedside, holding her hand and stroking her hair, I thought about that episode, the Mom, please episode, which ends with Rory coming home to find Lorelai in bed, fully dressed, rigid and silent with grief. Without a word, Rory climbs into bed next to her, stroking her hair. I had never, not once, seen my mother cry, just as I had never had a real conversation, a conversation of depth and substance, with her; she had never, not once, talked to me about the children she'd lost before my birth—my sister and brother—or about the trials she'd endured with my eldest sister, forever scarred by the deaths of her siblings, and, further, by my mother's refusal to talk with her about it, to grieve with her, to consider their loss shared, rather than singular; nor had she ever talked to me about my own life, never asked me why I married a man I didn't love, or how I got up the nerve to leave him for one I did, or anything at all about the texture of my days as a writer, nothing, nothing except, "Have you replaced your kitchen cabinets?" and "Are you still driving that Honda?"

Now, holding my mother's warm hand, swollen from the painkillers dripping into her arm, all the anger I'd held for her—the anger of that little girl—vanished; all I wanted was my mother back, not a Lorelai version of my mother, who allowed me access to her soul, but my actual mother, who had been a great mother, a wonderful mother, in the only way she knew how. I told her everything, everything she'd never asked me. The doctor had walked in on me reminiscing about a childhood trip to Hawaii. "Hearing is the last sense to go," he told me, kindly. "She can hear everything you say." And so I sat and talked and talked. I asked her everything I'd ever wanted to ask her, though it was too late for her to tell me about the small city in the Adirondacks in which she'd grown up, too late for her to tell me about working the hat counter at Lord & Taylor just after the war, too late for her to tell me who she really was beneath the elegantly tailored suits and the perfectly applied Chanel Rouge Gabrielle, behind the calculated pleasantness of her habitual expression. In my childhood, my teen years, if I had come home to find my mother in bed, fully clothed, frozen with sorrow, her world collapsed, I would have been shocked. Phyllis Rakoff, letting her emotions get in the way. In the way of being a mother, in the only way she knew how, which was to pretend she had no emotions. But now, as I talked, her face responded to everything I said, her eyebrows rising in astonishment, her mouth forming a semblance of a smile. "I love you so much, Mom," I told her, over and over.

At the beginning of the second season Rory asks Lorelai, "Do you think you and Grandma could ever talk about all the things you've gone through?" "No," Lorelai tells her. "I've tried. I've tried my whole life. But my mother and I, we speak a different language." For years, I thought *Gilmore Girls* changed my life in that it allowed me to be my actual self, my earnest, bookish self, without embarrassment or shame. And for many more years, I thought it changed my life by showing me how to be a mother in the way I wanted to be. Nearly a quarter century since I first turned on the television and found two brunettes speaking a language I thought specific to me and my little world, it changed my life again, in that it showed me that—as Lorelai slowly, slowly discovers herself—perhaps my mother and I spoke not different languages but simply variant dialects of the same tongue: love.

Everything Softens

Life and Death in Stars Hollow

Rand Richards Cooper

I'll put it right up front: I'm a *Gilmore Girls* refusenik. My nay-saying makes me an outlier in this collection of essays—and a pariah in my own *Gilmore*-worshipping family. Rarely do my wife and our high school teenager like me less than when I am volubly not liking those charming, fey, flippant-yet-soulful Gilmore girls. Who hasn't on occasion been daunted by the exercise in Venn diagramming that is family TV watching? Molly rejects TV series whose violence is too crass or whose human prospect too bleak—shows like *Succession* or *Big Little Lies*, where everyone is vile. I, meanwhile, can't always hang in with cheerful comedies. Larkin, our seventeen-year-old, has fewer exclusions—and so she and I will binge on the gritty nineties prison drama *Oz*, while she and Molly might chuckle through *The Good Place* or *The Great British Baking Show*.

Or *Gilmore Girls*.

It's not surprising that I have never felt at home in Stars Hollow. My favorite shows are usually dramas, and in movies I shy away from highly stylized directors, like Wes Anderson and Quentin Tarantino, whose work is an acquired taste. *Gilmore Girls* is an acquired taste that for two decades I failed to acquire, even as the two people closest to me were endlessly indulging it, devouring the show over and over—exuberant *Gilmore* gluttons, in the face of whose delight my own refusal seemed like pure churlishness. And it's true that I rarely feel as mean, in a TV-related way at least, as I do when saying no yet again to their invitation to get chummy with Rory and Lorelai and Jake.

OK, I mean, Luke. You see? The show brings out something malicious in me. "That's Jake with the cap, right?" I'll say, walking by the living room as they're watching. And this is only the beginning of my *Gilmore* peevishness. To whatever extent Lauren Graham's portrayal of Sarah Braverman in *Parenthood*—a show I liked—imported an essence of Lorelai Gilmore, I treated it as a small rotten spot in an otherwise sweet piece of fruit, and carefully ate around it. Similarly, or perhaps inversely, I get a cheap thrill out of seeing Graham play the slutty bartender in *Bad Santa*—as if somehow it constitutes an inter-series besmirching of Lorelai. These are not pretty sentiments. Yet Molly and Larkin remain ever hopeful. "Come on," they'll say as they sit watching the goings-on

in Stars Hollow (they are on their third go-round). "Give it
another chance!" They seem to believe there's something in it,
and in me, that will mesh, if only I will stop being so stubborn
and let it happen.

I actually have watched a fair amount of *Gilmore Girls* over
the years, just from being nearby while it is on—absorbing it
passively, like secondhand smoke. (Sorry, there I go again!)
Molly and Larkin scoff at the notion that I know the show from
these bits and pieces, like claiming you know a restaurant's
food by smelling its aroma from the street. And so, to refine
my sense of what master chef Amy Sherman-Palladino cooked
up in the *Gilmore* kitchen two decades ago—and figure out what
exactly it is that I'm allergic to in it—I recently watched my way
through a bunch of episodes.

Quickly I reacquainted myself with the show's deadpan
comedy, which reminded me that *Gilmore Girls* debuted just
two years after *Seinfeld* ended. In the first episode I watched,
season 2's "Teach Me Tonight," Rory and Lorelai comment on
the new checkout guy at the grocery store. "Hey, look," Lorelai
says, "new bag boy. Wow, he does the jar twirl. Very impressive." Then her rumination turns mock-sinister. "The jar
twirl, the double bagging, the 'Have a nice day, ma'am!' to
every customer—he's a snake in the grass." It's easy to imagine
Jerry speaking these exact words to Elaine, elevating a triv-
ial observation to mock-importance, in the best show-about-
nothing fashion. Ditto the back-and-forth, in another episode,
between Lorelai and a date, discussing the mysteries of Host-
ess Sno Balls ("Who makes these? Why are they shaped like a

boob? How did the decision to use coconut occur?"). I always loved this kind of thing when Jerry and Elaine did it. With Lorelai, not so much. But why not? Why relish how Elaine and Jerry remain perpetual adolescents, then demand that Lorelai grow up? I guessed it had to do with a sense of role confusion in *Gilmore Girls'* central relationship. Rory is Lorelai's daughter, after all, not her fellow Gen-X slacker.

"Lorelai is a paradox," Molly commented when we talked about it between episodes. "It's true that a parent's job is not to be her child's friend. But you have to remember that there's not that many years between them. If you have a child when you are a child, there's a very different feel to it. I have empathy for how and why she's Rory's friend."

"Best friend," Larkin added.

Parent and kid as best friends: that shouldn't be a deal-breaker for someone who grew up watching *The Rifleman* and *The Courtship of Eddie's Father*. Maybe it wasn't the Lorelai relationship itself that grated on me, I thought, but the language in which it is conducted—that hallmark *Gilmore Girls* dialogue. *Gilmore*-speak is a curious mixture of speed, overdetermined grammar, abundant irony, rampant cultural referencing, a tamped-down tonal range, and more than a dash of cutesiness. Above all, it is maximal, with words crammed into every nook and cranny.

Take this bit of dialogue from "Teach Me Tonight." Rory has suffered a fractured wrist in a car accident, with her love interest Jess driving, and at the end of a very trying day Lorelai tucks her into bed—a big blue cast on Rory's arm—and launches into a breathless barrage:

LORELAI: OK, so you've got your TV, your books, your magazines, your refreshments, you have your CD player and your assorted CDs, Stan Freberg, Ash—you have Sinéad O'Connor, because when life really gets you down, Sinéad's really the one to teach you some perspective—and you have a pad and paper in case you start to want to write that Great American novel, and over here you have a tiny but annoying bell, in case there's something you need that you don't have, and you want to summon the common but lively house wench, who will promptly leave all her talking mice and come to fetch the Contessa whatever she might require.

RORY: I think what the Contessa requires right now is sleep.

One might imagine writing Lorelai's dialogue in this torrential manner in order to convey the pent-up anxiety of a mother venting over her daughter's mishap—and to amp up the intensity of language for the episode's key moment. But the breathless barrage is not a mode reserved for key moments in *Gilmore Girls*; rather, it's the m.o. of the show, its default idiom. Sookie talks that way, worrying aloud on the morning of her wedding; Michel, Lorelai's high-strung French majordomo, talks that way when insisting to Lorelai that he won't work more overtime at the Dragonfly Inn.

And every time someone does it, I squirm; it makes me feel trapped. You know how certain novelists can plaster a page with wall-to-wall words in an intimidating way—David Foster Wallace sometimes did this—so that you find yourself desperately wanting more white space? That's how I feel about dialogue in *Gilmore Girls*. More silence, please! These are supposed to be human beings, after all. "I just got so tired of how they sound," a friend of mine said, explaining why she stopped watching the show.

It's not lost on me, as a writer, that "how people actually talk" is not the be-all and end-all of dialogue. As Molly likes to point out, *Gilmore Girls'* dialogue evokes the William Powell/Myrna Loy Nick and Nora movies of the 1940s, which refashioned Dashiell Hammett's hard-boiled noir into a bantering repartee, in the process adding flirtatious verve to the Hollywood picture of marriage. Do we blame Nick and Nora for not sounding "real"? Do we hold it against Spencer Tracy and Katharine Hepburn? Every work of narrative art sets rules that might at first seem strange, and the experience of engaging with it involves accustoming ourselves bit by bit to these rules, accepting the story in the way it is asking to be told.

But with *Gilmore Girls*, I've just never quite been able to get there. It's telling that among the main characters, I'm drawn to Lorelai's mother, Emily. Is that partly because actress Kelly Bishop played Sheila in *A Chorus Line*, which I saw as a teenager, and sang the luminous song "At the Ballet"? No doubt!

But it's also because Emily is the one major character who doesn't do the Stars Hollow rat-a-tat-tat-alogue. Rather the opposite. Aiming her owl-like stare at Lorelai, she repeatedly dishes out moments of baleful silence—to my relief. In "I Can't Get Started," the final episode of season 2, Lorelai and Rory, visiting Emily in Hartford, indulge a Seinfeldian riff on "oy" and "poodle," musing over what funny words they are and joking that "if you put them together, you'd have a great new catchphrase: 'Oy with the poodles already!'"

"Oh for God's sake," says Emily, hovering nearby. "Be quiet!"

Yes, I understand that Emily is as close to a villain as you will get in *Gilmore Girls*. She's judgy, crotchety, and cold. But in putting the clamps on her daughter's runaway verbiage, she speaks for me. Or rather, is quiet for me.

My wife and child proved articulate advocates for their favorite show. In our conversations they insisted that I was pigeonholing *Gilmore Girls* as light comedy, that there were dimensions and tones I was missing. "It has an emotional core to it," Larkin said. "There are scenes that stick with you." "I love it that the wit and the clever referencing are so lighthearted and fun and fast," Molly added, "but the show doesn't avoid darkness. It can turn on a dime into a beautifully rendered scene of real conflict, between characters with real depth. There's a way in which it toggles between those two states."

As I learned via my ten-pack *Gilmore* sampler, often that pivot, that toggling action, involves an expression on Lorelai's face. "A House Is Not a Home" (season 5, episode 22) inter-weaves the comedy of a cycling race that swamps Luke's diner with the farce of Lane and her buffoonish bandmates, then adds Rory's troubles at Yale and her surging anxiety about her future, culminating in her arguing bitterly with Lorelai and seeking refuge with her grandparents.

The episode ends with Lorelai standing in the yard out-side her parents' guesthouse, watching through the win-dows as Rory glumly unpacks her stuff—the usual smiling liveliness drained from Lorelai's face, leaving only a look of anguished parental love. A similar moment occurs at the end of season 2's "I Can't Get Started," when Lorelai has to shift instantly from having her heart broken by her ex, Chris, to serving as bridesmaid for Sookie—marching toward the nuptials, posy bouquet in hand, while struggling to hide her own heartbreak.

These poignant moments are a popular feature of the series; google "saddest *Gilmore Girls* episode" and you'll find a dozen sites where fans list their favorite weepisodes. Yet in the over-all run of the show, they are few and far between. More typi-cal is the facetious sprightliness of another episode I watched, "Ted Koppel's Big Night Out," in which Lorelai and Rory attend the Yale-Harvard game with Lorelai's parents, followed by Lorelai's date with Jason, a young partner of her father's. The date goes badly, including some competitive sulking at a fast-food place (Lorelai: "I'm not gonna eat if you're not gonna eat." Jason: "What is this, junior high?"), but is ultimately salvaged when the two go to a supermarket and buy Cap'n Crunch and other junk food from their childhood. After the date, Lorelai calls Rory to recap:

LORELAI: Sorry for bailing earlier.

RORY: No problem, you just owe me the gory details.

LORELAI: I think I might like him.

RORY: Just remember, you're sleeping with every single person he has ever slept with.

LORELAI: Thank you for that!

RORY: Call me tomorrow.

LORELAI: You got it!

I find myself wincing at this exchange, with its cloying cheerfulness and adolescent teasing—and there I go again, disliking the very aspects of the show that endear it to fans. To cadge the classic relationship breakup line, the problem isn't the show, it's me. It seems there's hardly a feature of *Gilmore Girls* that I have not liked elsewhere—as long as men are doing it. Take that "stilted" dialogue I always complain about. Well, what about David Mamet's characters in *Glengarry Glen Ross*, those desperate salesmen, with their bulky soliloquies of belligerence and dread? Their explosions of angst don't sound at all like real people talking. But I admire Mamet's dialogue; it seems "real" to me, if not literally, then in its ability to convey some essence of—well, of maleness.

Is my persistent churlishness regarding *Gilmore Girls* finally just a form of misogyny? I remember the feminist excitement about *Thelma & Louise* and how a classic male genre (the buddy movie, the road movie) was being hijacked for women's use, reimagined through a female gaze. I wonder if, at base, what I resist in *Gilmore Girls* is precisely that female gaze, the way in which all problems—from the success or failure of a date, to the challenges of pursuing a career in a male-dominated profession, to the never-ending issues with your mother—are conceived, scripted, and delivered by women.

And for women. Yes, there are shows that appeal to men and women equally—*Friday Nights Lights*, say, or *The Office*. But more often a show skews one way or another, and it's no surprise to learn who exactly has been loving *Gilmore Girls* for the past two decades. A study by the social media research company Brandwatch found that the show's fan base was and is "overwhelmingly female"—and even today, decades later, it remains the second-most-watched TV show among eighteen-to-thirty-four-year-old women. Not my demographic.

So while I'd like to be able to pivot here, in the best *Gilmore Girls* manner—to turn on a dime and take this essay to a greater depth and a subtler tone—it isn't going to involve me discovering my inner Gilmore girl. Try as I might, I did not succeed in vaulting over the gender divide and landing happily in Stars Hollow.

Yet there is a pivot, and it comes in the memory of someone who did vault over that divide. Among the nation of *Gilmore* loyalists you might not expect to find a gruff, bearded, chain-smoking, pot-smoking forty-year-old fisherman and Grateful Dead fanatic. But that was my brother-in-law, Wes. And the story of how he and Molly—his seven-years-younger sister—

watched *Gilmore Girls* together in the waning months of Wes's life is a cherished story in our family. Who exactly are the boundary-crossing guys who love *Gilmore Girls*? Let me introduce you to an unforgettable one.

Wes was a character. Dyslexic in an era before learning specialists, he struggled in school, eventually dropping out partway through tenth grade. In subsequent years he drifted, partying with friends who'd gone on to college, taking housepainting and handyman jobs, attending dozens of Grateful Dead concerts. Wes loved dogs, had bad luck with women, reviled snobs with high-blown educations, made beautiful handcrafted fishing poles, and looked like a member of ZZ Top. He struggled with alcohol addiction and could be a fearsome drunk. A vivid storyteller, he loved nothing more than to regale friends with raucous narratives, laughing boisterously within a haze of cigarette smoke. He was wildly profane. The very first time I met him, at a family picnic, I was dating Molly; we were still in that egregious public-display-of-affection phase, and after half an hour of watching us, Wes turned to me, waved his cigarette, and said, "Jesus, just take her behind a bush and bang her, will you?" I was agog. Could this wild man really be the brother of the sensitive, diplomatic, bookish, and quiet person I was in love with?

In the spring of 2002, Wes experienced a persistent, nagging cough. He hated going to doctors, and went in a mood of dark pessimism, expecting the worst. Relax, we told him; who gets lung cancer at forty?

Me, he said grimly. And he was right.

His death was protracted and brutal. When my own mother died of lung cancer four years later, she was a slender, frail eighty-year-old, and the disease proceeded quickly; but Wes was young and strong. It took three years, with brutal treatments and one remission that lasted just long enough to raise his hopes and then, via an aggressive recurrence, cruelly dash them. Soon after getting that grim news, he left his apartment and moved in with my mother-in-law Kathy, occupying a tiny room on the ground floor of her small house. As the months passed and his condition worsened, he stopped going out, stopped receiving visits from concerned friends. Wes did not want to talk about what was happening to him. His fear was primal, his denial resolute. Sometimes he would simply pull the covers up over his head, as if he could make it all just go away.

Once a week Molly would make the hour-long drive after work to visit her desperately ill brother. Wes would try to get some food down, and the two would watch TV. Monster truck competitions, a show about a guy building motorcycles in California, anything about snakes, sharks, or storms: Wes's favorites were deep-grained guy stuff. With one exception. "He had a little secret other side to him," Molly explains. "One day I called and asked what he was doing, and he said he was watching *Gilmore Girls*. I had never heard of it. He said, 'You would love this show. You have to watch it.' So we did." Eventually Molly began to plan her trips for Tuesdays—*Gilmore* night—to spend time with Wesley, Lorelai, and Rory.

What exactly was the appeal of this ultimate girls' show to my roughneck brother-in-law?

Wes wasn't the kind of guy who sat around discussing what he loved about TV shows. But he clearly enjoyed spending time with *Gilmore Girls'* colorful, lovable weirdos; he vibed with the island-of-misfit-toys quality that the show so gently puts forth. There were more direct affinities, too. Like Luke, Wes was capable of falling in love and never doing anything about it—longing for a woman from a safe distance rather than risking a possibly ham-fisted overture. And like Lorelai, he grew up a black sheep in a fairly well-to-do family. "Lorelai is brought up amid wealth and privilege, and leaves that whole scene behind," Molly says. "She's a rebel who is downwardly mobile, and the idea that she lifts her middle finger to those parents, strikes out on her own and makes her own way in the world—that was deeply, deeply appealing to Wes." It was something he had done himself, in his own way.

Looking back, I think Wes loved the show for other reasons as well—situational reasons still poignant to me, twenty years later. They reflect the nature of Stars Hollow and its cozy small-town fantasy. "*Gilmore Girls* has a slightly fairy-tale-ish feeling to it," Larkin said. "You're entering this little world where there are problems, but it's all OK somehow. Of all the places for a pregnant sixteen-year-old to run away and end up, there's not really an imaginably better place than this. There's something that's just very comforting about the show." "It's idealized," Molly said. "Stars Hollow is this dreamy little place where people are ridiculous, and sometimes mad at each other, but it's gentle. That's the fairy-tale part of it, and the comfort part. There's a forgivingness to it. And it offers what all good stories offer, which is the resolution that life doesn't always offer."

Forgivingness. Acceptance. Comfort. Resolution. *Gilmore Girls* held out a generous welcome for a person like Wes, whose path through life had been crooked and full of missteps. Larkin elaborated on this central theme of the show. "Anyone who has felt like a misfit in their family savors the idea that that misfitism could lead you to a place like Stars Hollow, where your kid would get raised by a whole community and you would know everyone, and everyone would be a bit strange, and they would all love you for your strangeness. In a metaphorical sense, I think it's what everyone wishes they had from their hometown. I would like to live there!"

She and Molly talked about the rituals of community and of family life that the show portrays, from the annual Revolutionary War battle reenactment that Luke is so bored by, to Lorelai telling Rory about her birth every year on her birthday, to Lorelai's thrill every winter at the first snow, reiterated in multiple episodes over the years. I myself was captivated by the moment in "Love and War and Snow," in season 1, where Lorelai raises her bedroom window one night in early winter, leans outside, and inhales deeply—sensing something in the cold night air and gazing up with a look of expectant delight. "Can't you smell it?" she asks Rory. "Everything's magical when it snows." As the two cuddle up under a blanket on the couch—keeping the window open—Lorelai tells her daughter about the charmed role snow has played in her life, how the best things have happened during snowstorms, from her first kiss to Rory's own birth.

Later in the episode, she takes a walk through Stars Hollow, the village sparkly with newly fallen snow, as Ella Fitzgerald croons "Someone to Watch Over Me" in the background. When Wes died, in August 2005, *Gilmore Girls* had just finished the fifth of its eventual seven seasons. "This was the live-time TV era, before streaming," Molly recalls. "Wes never saw the show all the way through. He never knew that Luke and Lorelai got married." But the last episode he would have seen, in the spring of 2005—the season 5 finale I mentioned earlier, "A House Is Not a Home"—closes with Lorelai spontaneously proposing to Luke. So Wes would have had at least an inkling that things would work out, and that his stand-in as awkward suitor would prevail.

The most urgent moments in our lives contain powerful opposites—laughter and sorrow, togetherness and aloneness, all mingled up with one another. I think about my wife and her dying brother, there in that tiny room filled with dread, taking in the rituals of life in Stars Hollow and turning it all into their own weekly ritual; I picture the two of them laughing together in pleasure. I like to think that Wes found both respite and refuge in that fairy-tale village, with Lorelai and Rory, Luke and Sookie and Lane and Kirk and all the rest. A fisherman and boatman, Wes loved weather, and over the years would often call us in elated excitement at the approach of a storm.

I imagine him watching one of *Gilmore Girls'* first-snow

episodes on a winter night, looking out the window of his sickroom—buoyed, as I imagine it, by the timelessness of the seasons, with its intimation of a reality above and beyond our human moment, and by a nature that soothes us with its beauty. And finding in it at least a passing moment of serenity. "The world changes when it snows," Lorelai says. "It gets quiet. Everything softens."

Where You Lead (I Will Follow)

Gilmore Girls and the Soundtrack of Emotional Dependency

Katie Moulton

In my teens and early twenties, everyone told me and Mama that we reminded them of "real-life Gilmore girls." "You know that show, with the mom and daughter? They're like best friends, you know, quick, clever. You two are just like them!" Aunts and friends and strangers at Home Depot commented on our duo's dynamism: our closeness, our banter, our road trips and hijinks. Linda and Katie, a regular Lorelai and Rory, deeply intertwined and self-contained in our cozy culture of two.

Gilmore Girls ran from 2000 to 2007, a family-friendly out-lier amid the WB's slate of dramas featuring relentlessly self-serious teenagers. The series run also spanned the precise years that I was fourteen to twenty-one. I was just one year younger than the fictional Rory. I was also a student journalist and valedictorian of my high school, headed for an East Coast university far beyond the ken of my family. Mama, like Lore-lai, was a people person, a charmer and problem-solver who treated her job in big-box retail like it was luxury hospitality. Basically, I was smart and Mama was fun. I was more fun when buoyed on her currents, and she was so, so proud of me. As fans of the show, we took the comparison as it was intended: a huge compliment.

We were best friends, and that wasn't cringe. She didn't try to be a "cool mom," but nonetheless, my longtime friends and boyfriends came to concerts with us and invited her to the bar for twenty-first birthdays. They laughed and gossiped with her, called her "Mama Tan," a Midwest-cockney transmutation of my own nickname. They accepted that I would confide in her first and checked in on her when I was away. Her friends asked her how I was, and mine asked me how she was. They knew that asking about Mama was the same as asking about me at my core. Like comfort-show *Gilmore Girls*, our relationship was like a small, glowing campfire people gathered around to warm their hands. That glimmering vision reflected back to us, and we stoked the fire of "the two of us," sang its song.

The characters of Stars Hollow are inextricable from its soundtrack—strummy songs woven like garland around the gazebo pillars. The opening notes of the *Gilmore Girls* universe are the chiming guitar chords of "There She Goes" by the English jangle-pop band the La's. In the pilot episode, the camera greets Lorelai, brightly lit in autumnal knits, navigating the small-town sidewalks, at home in the space and in herself.

The song was released in 1988, became a hit in 1990, and then became a hit *again* in 1999, when it was covered by American Christian soft-alt-rock band Sixpence None the Richer. This rejuvenation served as a natural bridge between generations of viewers and the show's main characters, relevant to millennial adolescents of the moment and Gen-X memories of their young adulthood. "There She Goes" has been described by nineties pop-rock hero Noel Gallagher of Oasis as his favorite song of its era, and by 'oos pop-rock hero Ben Gibbard of Death Cab for Cutie as a "perfect song," so simple and timeless that you feel it has always existed. Its overriding factor is wistful sweetness. It's all momentary longing—a song with *no verses*, only a chorus, repeated with changing lyrics, plus a bridge. "There—*she*—goes," the singer lilts, lifting high on the middle *she*, before gently setting down again, the echo of "There she goes again" coming from his mind or his buddies or their small town, "chasing down my lane." Band member John Byrne said, "It's just a love song about a girl you never talk to."

In the opening scene of *Gilmore Girls*, we the viewers understand that *that girl* is both Lorelai and Rory, bouncing around Stars Hollow: pretty, witty, and self-assured, but utterly contained within themselves and, critically, contained by each other. Their quirky repartee will delight you even as—and maybe because—half the time you don't know what they're talking about. That self-containment—a.k.a. their resistance to external need—becomes the core of their charm.

Over the years, "There She Goes" gathered a reputation as a secret ode to heroin due to lyrics that describe "she" wreaking havoc on the singer's *brain* and *vein*, yet healing his *pain*. Perhaps this conspiracy is supported by the song structure itself. We just described the song's chorus-chorus-chorus-chorus as enacting the overflow-immediacy of perceiving a crush, but maybe it's illustrating a different high, and the cyclical trap of depending on that rush, the need to exist in that present over and over.

What else did people say about Mama and me? What did they see? That we were alone together. That we, too, like Lorelai and Rory, had lost the third person who made our family.

When I was growing up, one of Mama's favorite quips was, "She got her daddy's looks, but thank *God* she got my personality." I glowed with that compliment.

At the end of the third season of *Gilmore Girls*, my dad died. He was beautiful, sensitive, funny, charismatic, really goddamn smart, and so lost. He was a former record-store manager and music fanatic who shared his records and books with me. He had struggled with alcoholism, addiction, and depression for as long as I could remember. In that year leading up to his unexpected death, I was sixteen. I was falling in love with my first boyfriend, lying to stay out late and then confessing all to Mama, getting straight A's but lashing out at friends and crying at my desk, face in my hands. Like Rory, I thought I was a shoo-in for editor in chief of the newspaper, but my wise advisor gave it to the student who was less divided in her focus. I went to Alateen meetings, practiced saying "one day at a time" and "first things first," and still seethed at my dad after school. Nothing we did changed anything, but we couldn't stop. He'd stopped working, then stopped going to meetings, stopped leaving his room. Sometimes disappeared. I was pretty sure my dad thought we'd be better off without him. But he couldn't make himself leave, and he couldn't escape himself.

In fall 2002, six months before he died, Mama and I watched the episode with the dance marathon, "They Shoot Gilmores, Don't They?" I already knew the reference. I'd watched the Sydney Pollack film *They Shoot Horses, Don't They?* with my parents as a kid. Made in 1969, based on a Depression-era novel, it's basically an absurdist existentialist horror film about how the whole system—including life itself—is rigged against us. I mostly remembered the film's ending: Jane Fonda, tough and gorgeous, on the ghostly pier at the end, asking the calf-eyed boy to help her kill herself.

But what I remembered most about the *Gilmore Girls* version of a catastrophic dance marathon is that Lorelai and Rory are partners. When fatigue and tension boil over and the boys leave, they're left holding each other.

Who among us gets out of adolescence alive? Who can leave their parents whole? The day after my dad died, I turned seventeen. Sixteen-going-on-seventeen, the end of high school, a critical moment of child-parent separation. But that's not what happened.

Mama and I had attended Al-Anon meetings together in a church basement, at least until one of the other members gently suggested that I should maybe go to a different meeting, maybe even one for kids. We'd both learned terms like *enabler* and *codependency* and *family illness*. I repeated "the three C's"—*I didn't cause it, I can't control it, I can't cure it*—and I tried to believe it about my dad's addiction. But when it came to Mama—her desolation, her emotional caretaking—I believed the opposite: I was the only one who could do anything about it. When we might have pulled apart, I fused more closely than ever to Mama.

The theme song that plays over the opening credits of *Gilmore Girls* is "Where You Lead" by Carole King. I have long loved this song from my parents' generation, a B-list track off an all-time great record (*Tapestry*, 1971) by one of the all-time great singer-songwriters. It's a jaunty folk-pop record featuring electric piano, lively drums, a sly guitar line, and background vocals from the legendary Merry Clayton, cooing part doo-wop, part gospel. Over it all, King makes bold declarations of devotion in her warm, scratchy, marvelous voice. Wherever the beloved leads, wherever they say, she'll follow.

When I moved across the country for college, family and acquaintances asked Mama, "How can you let her go so far away?" I did feel guilty, afraid to leave her on her own. I called her multiple times a day. I wanted her to know that I was out there, the same, reflecting her, thinking of her. I called when

I felt overwhelmed by my classes or shamed by another hazy hungover noon, and Mama gave me permission to opt out, forgave me anything I confessed or didn't. And then she reminded me who I was: her girl who could do anything. I called, too, when nothing was wrong but everything was. I didn't have to say his name. She knew. We were bound together by our huge, unending grief. We'd both been there. We were still there.

"I'll be there," King sings. All her love has to do is call, and she'll jump the next train. I went home for every break, holiday, in between—taking the subway from campus to a train to a bus to a plane. In the summers, we took road trips together—meandering across the Midwest, tracing the Mississippi to the Florida Gulf Coast, journeying through Yellowstone, returning with tales and inside jokes. Once, Mama and I followed Route 66 all the way from St. Louis to the Grand Canyon and back. We hit every desert diner and cheesy trinket shop; she drove and I called numbers in the Triple-A book to get a motel room in whatever town we'd reach by nightfall. I made mix CDs for our trip, featuring, naturally, "Where You Lead" by Carole King. It was a promise that I would never really leave.

When we made it to the edge of the famous abyss, we stood side by side, our hands linked tight. "Go out there a little ways," Mama said, "so I can take your picture." I scrambled out on the ledge—precarious, but not too far—and swiveled around to beam back at her camera.

As *Gilmore Girls* progressed and we all got older, I began to chafe against the fictional mother-daughter-sister-friend dynamic. I grew deeply uncomfortable with the reflection—

and the projections. I rewatched Lorelai give a toast at Rory's sixteenth birthday party, describing her daughter as "the one thing in my life that is always good, always sweet, and without whom I would have no reason to get up in the morning—my pal, Rory." I cringed, and then I got mad. Why did Lorelai define Rory only in relation to herself? While Lorelai can choose to treat Rory as her "pal" and emotional support and "the sensible one," Rory never gets to decide. And that last bit—"no reason to get up"—how's that for pressure?

I returned home again and again. After college, I moved back in with Mama. *There she goes.* Even as I longed for and held sacred the safety of our bond, I resented my role as a kind of parent. (*There she goes again.*) As the sole witness to her tears, the tender of her emotional tumult, the keeper of her hopes, answerable for any free-floating bad feeling.

I realized that "Where You Lead" was originally written as a song of nearly claustrophobic romantic devotion à la the Book of Ruth. While writing the song, King sent an almost-finished version to songwriter Toni Stern because she couldn't figure out the bridge. Stern apparently bristled at the song's "arguably servile stance" and wrote new lyrics that complicated the zealous fidelity with sharpness and nuance. She added the bridge, which seems to introduce a potential dispute and compromise: "But if you want to live in *fucking* New York City"—she will.

Even after the song was released, critics described the lyrics as "ingratiating," "romantically extreme," and even reinforcing gender stereotypes. A few years after the release of

Tapestry, King herself reevaluated the song and deemed its sentiments retrograde, even politically incorrect, and stopped performing it live.

I moved away, but not too far. Mama and I both fell in love again, and those loves lasted. When she married the man who had once been her high school boyfriend, I stood by her side. I gave a toast. I talked about *The Velveteen Rabbit*, the story that Mama and I have told each other over the years. "Real isn't how you are made," a wiser toy tells the tragic rabbit. "It's a thing that happens to you. When a child REALLY loves you, then you become Real." Our love had made each other real, I think I meant, and now his love made her a different kind of real. "Does it hurt?" the Rabbit asks. And the wiser toy, always truthful, says, "Sometimes."

I moved farther and farther away. I flew home less often. I lived in apartments in multiple cities that Mama never saw. We talked less frequently on the phone, each blaming the other for the growing distance. We couldn't square it. We were happy; we loved each other. We were on each end of the line. We knew what we were to each other. Why couldn't we hold it anymore?

She flew to a western city to celebrate my thirtieth birthday. At the party, she was tense, nervous about the cake she'd brought, unsure in the setting of my new life. She gave a toast. She told the stories of times I had been "bad": Once, as a toddler, I picked up a marble from a shop floor, and she marched me back into the mall to "confess" to the cashier. Another time, one teenage Friday, I came home to giddily recount pranking a friend's car with shaving cream and Silly String—and she made me wash the "vandalized" car by hand, at midnight, in front of my friend, who eventually started feeling bad for me. Her point was that I was innocent somehow, and that she was a kook. The toast was about her own self-consciousness, and this time, in the smoky blaze of her attention, the reflection of "the two of us" felt strangled and distorted. Later she cried on a sidewalk outside the bar, saying, "You don't look at me the same."

At this point in the essay, I'm casting about for a scene that crystallizes when and how things changed for Mama and my Lorelai-and-Rory kinship. That's the fiction of memoir, and the fiction of *Gilmore Girls*. Even in life, episodes string together chronologically, but there's no climactic blowup, no "I'm dropping out of Yale" in our ongoing story.

At this point in the essay, I'm doing anything other than typing (i.e., hosting all-day brunches, sweeping behind the toilet, volunteering for jury duty—that last one, actually good for writing). At this point, I'm interrogating friends with how they feel about Lorelai and Rory's relationship. "I was jealous," one pal says. "It seemed ideal." Her girlfriend chimes in, "I wasn't jealous, I think, because it just seemed so unrealistic."

At this point, I'm asking, *Is codependency even bad?* I'm enlisting my sweetheart to weigh in, and he is pausing the episode on Lorelai's birthday toast, exclaiming, "Did you see that shit?" But I'm asking the question aloud (while disinfecting the microwave): *Can codependency be beautiful? Can it be healthy? Is it something to admire or strive for?*

Codependency, it turns out, is a word that gets bandied about a lot these days but can't be diagnosed. What do we mean by *codependency*, a.k.a. what do *I* mean by it? The nonprofit Mental Health America lists seventeen characteristics of codependent people, and oh man, they all fit, including right at the very top: "an exaggerated sense of responsibility for the actions of others" and "the tendency to do anything to hold on to a relationship to avoid the feeling of abandonment."

I think of Lorelai in the pilot accusing Rory of misbehavior, the root of their first splintering fight: "Of course you would. After all, you're *me*." But her daughter is not her, of course she's not. Didn't cause, can't control, can't cure. But why doesn't this practiced detachment offer any solace, any freedom? Why would I tend and fight and tiptoe futilely rather than admit I can't fix it when Mama hurts? And why does "you're me" feel so good to hear?

I stopped watching *Gilmore Girls* around the time that Lorelai and Rory had a falling-out and didn't speak for nearly half a season. When I go back to the reruns, I start at the beginning. Sometimes I rage in irritation—every time Lorelai insists "this isn't you," every time Rory is upset because Lorelai is upset. But I'm not thinking about how the citizens of Stars Hollow should tune in to the potential harm of this topsy-turvy, codependent arrested-development, parent-child dynamic. I'm not feeling the confusion or the weight.

Most of all, I watch *Gilmore Girls* and think: I had that. I *had* that. And now I don't.

Mama and I still talk once a week, text in between. We're

kind to each other. We try to listen, to laugh. We give each other news and advice—most of the time, when asked. We try not to judge, but it's hard to remember that the person I'm talking to isn't me.

Sure, it's necessary to separate from our mothers. Yes, Mama and I did it too late and that made it hurt more. Somehow, we're both forever teenagers together, unable to retie ourselves in a way that makes sense.

It's a potent, long-lasting fantasy to be someone's everything. With great love, we—and by we, I mean *I*—never wish that we hadn't done it, hadn't known it. Knowing everything I know, I still want it back. If only for the chance to figure out the end before it comes for us. If I could have loved better, then I could have left better. Maybe we'd have been able to hold on to more of the way we were. Maybe that's a fantasy too. But since we're dealing in the very real fantasies we refer to as our memories, our loves, ourselves—I'll pose that question. What do I wish for Mama and me? What would I do differently?

What would Carole King do?

I had bridled at the submissive position of "Where You Lead" and the transference of devotion from romantic to parent-child. I listened again. I noticed a difference in the version playing over the *Gilmore Girls'* opening montage. It turns out King didn't just license the use of the song. Instead, she evolved the lyrics in the second half of the bridge. Those lines are about doubting she could ever be content with "just one man," but her revision opens other possibilities. She warns us that we never know how things turn out, but as long as we're together, "we can find a way."

Then King rerecorded the song as a duet with Louise Goffin, her own daughter.

If we can't make meaning, someone said, maybe we can make music. I have to work to see Mama as separate from myself, and to see us both as separate from the earlier versions of us. Maybe a rerecording is possible. A duet, familiar but with small necessary changes. This is my ongoing hope for me and Mama—to reimagine our song and to sing it better together and apart.

Many Coats of Many Colors

Nina de Gramont

People like to complain about television real estate, the unrealistic square footage of Manhattan apartments. But I prefer to talk about coats. TV characters, no matter their income, have many more coats than ordinary people. Take Buffy Summers, the teenage vampire slayer, who has a new and beautiful coat for every day of the week. And she lives in Southern California! In season 5 Buffy's mother dies, leaving behind her ruined finances. No wonder. She spent tens of thousands of dollars on her daughter's coats.

Lorelai Gilmore, who lives in Connecticut, has a more valid need for coats than Buffy Summers. But even for the Northeast, Lorelai's coat collection seems excessive. She has boiled wool coats of every color, length, and style. The same goes for down coats, and leather jackets. She has an enviable collection of barn jackets, lined and unlined. She has duffle coats and peacoats. Every coat you ever wished for is somewhere in her closet, which must be like Hermione Granger's beaded handbag, space magically immaterial to content.

It's important to be clear, here at the start: I love Lorelai Gilmore. I love her like a best friend or sister—whose every character flaw I know, understand, and forgive, even if she does have too many coats.

In the early 2000s, when *Gilmore Girls* first aired, I may have been aware of its existence but never watched a single episode. My husband and I, both writers, were cobbling together an artist's life, always lacking for cash, packing up and moving between borrowed houses and rented apartments. We seldom owned a television. In 2002, David and I lived in Cambridge, a winter frigid enough that whenever we ate at our favorite Indian restaurant, the manager

remembered I got cold easily and sent a space heater over to our table. I was pregnant at the time and owned exactly one maternity coat, a black knee-length puffer from the Gap. It may have been the only piece of maternity clothing I bought—all my others were hand-me-downs.

You may have noticed that in the middle of a paragraph describing myself as broke, I admit to being enough of a regular at a Cambridge restaurant (the Bombay Club, RIP) that they had a system in place to keep me warm. Consider that a confession: I am as reckless with money as Lorelai Gilmore.

My romance with Stars Hollow bloomed in 2014, when

it began streaming on Netflix. My Gap maternity coat had long been passed on to someone else, and the human who'd necessitated it was now eleven years old. My daughter and I have always been incredibly close. "You love me an abnormal amount," she recently accused, and—second confession—I admit that's true. From the first episode we watched together, H and I saw ourselves in Lorelai and Rory.

That winter David was mostly on the road, researching a book. In the evenings, H and I would get takeout and watch *Gilmore Girls*. We raced through all seven seasons in three months. Compared to the southern city where we both felt like expats, Stars Hollow—with its Victorian houses, snowy winters, and embracive, eclectic neighbors—felt like native territory. We wanted it to be real.

But how could it be real, with all that beautiful, abundant outerwear? In the pilot episode, Lorelai wears exactly one coat, a beautiful ankle-length camel hair. I will not count her blazers, or dusters, or any kind of sweater. I am only counting coats. At the same time, Lorelai's blazers are not irrelevant. She needs to dress professionally for her job managing the Independence Inn, and she does, in gorgeous suits of varied material—silk, wool, herringbone.

Wouldn't the money she'd need to spend on blazers significantly cut into her coat budget?

Season 1 of *Gilmore Girls* boasts a whopping twenty-one episodes. In episode 13, Rory presses Lorelai to donate clothing to a "charity rummage sale." Looking through her bedroom closet, Lorelai insists she has nothing to donate. "I wear it all," she says, and I believe her.

Here is a likely incomplete list of coats Lorelai wears in season 1, excluding the aforementioned camel hair: Belted charcoal wool overcoat. Button-down charcoal wool overcoat. Black leather motorcycle jacket. Red leather jacket. Red-lined black fleece jacket. Classic jean jacket. Tailored black leather jacket with lapels. Fleece-lined jean jacket. Black button-down wool overcoat. Powder blue waist-length puffer (anyone living in New England needs at least one puffer). Chocolate brown button-down overcoat. Black waist-length puffer lined and trimmed with fur (we assume faux, Rory would never allow the real thing). Beige fleece jacket. Tailored jean jacket with lapels. Waist-length light beige overcoat. Forest green corduroy jacket.

I picture the closet in Lorelai's front hall, so full she can barely push the door closed. It's only season 1. We've just met the Gilmores. Maybe all these coats were collected over the past decade, lovingly cared for to always look spotless and brand new.

I want to believe in something that will make the coats seem true. I want to believe in Stars Hollow.

As a child, I went to private school. My parents could afford it but just barely, and I always felt poor compared to my classmates, who lived in homes that looked a lot like Emily and Richard Gilmore's. I now recognize my childhood as insanely privileged, but of course I didn't at the time. I only compared my family's resources to what seemed like the limitless wealth of my classmates.

When I was in seventh grade, my grandmother sent me a winter coat. It was a hideous puffer, bright crossing-guard orange, with white chevron stripes on either sleeve. "You would not be caught dead in this coat," I told my mother when we took it out of the box. She did not refute this, nor did she buy me a replacement. Every morning as I left for school she would call out, "Take your coat!"

I don't think I ever pulled that coat onto my body. Who knows if it even fit? Every day I would carry it to school, where I'd shove it into my locker and shiver through the day as I walked from one building to another in the northern New Jersey winter.

When my daughter started kindergarten I enrolled her in a private school, as if I'd learned nothing from my own past. Like Lorelai, I had to go to my parents for help with the tuition. This was 2008, and the stock market crash soon made it impossible for my long-retired parents to bankroll a second generation of private school.

It would have been fiscally responsible to move H into the perfectly adequate public school where we were zoned. But fiscal responsibility has never been David's and my strong suit. The tuition was modest enough that I thought we wouldn't be the only parents scraping together the money. In the pickup line my heart would leap with optimism when I saw what looked like an economy car, but it always turned out to be a Prius, or belong to a babysitter. All the people who would have had to cobble tuition together were smart enough to use the schools their taxes paid for. I joked about making a coffee table book called "Private School Playdates," with photographs of our dented little Scion parked in front of one glorious mansion after another. H didn't notice the income disparity until deep into first grade, when she said: "All the other kids have a lot more shoes than I do."

In early 2015, I posted on Facebook about TV characters and their unlikely plethora of coats. Enough people commented, and enough people were on the *Gilmore Girls* binge bandwagon, that the comments turned into a conversation about Lorelai and her spending habits. "Lorelai is terrible with money," one friend wrote. Consensus was that if Lorelai didn't spend so much on eating out every day, and buying junk food for movie nights, she could have paid for Chilton herself.

Americans are puritanical about how those with modest means spend money. The rich can waste millions on yachts and endless summer homes because it's theirs to spend. But when someone who's struggling buys a mocha latte, the whole world wags its fingers. David and I went deep into debt paying for private elementary school. And the truth is, we might have been able to swing tuition without debt if we'd abandoned Starbucks and restaurants. In the realm of private school, H's elementary school was not that expensive. From 2008 to 2015, on the yearly payment plan, it ran just under $600 a month. But Chilton? According to the Education Data Initiative, Connecticut has the highest private school tuitions in the country.

Chilton's architecture and grounds are based on Choate

Rosemary Hall, whose tuition for a day student in 2001 ran $20,302. The difference between groceries from Doose's Market and takeout from Al's Pancake World was never going to cover that cost.

Lorelai is not only a single mother, she was a teenage mother. She has a demanding full-time job. At only thirty-two, she's a homeowner. Although she has no household help, her place always looks clean. Let her have her takeout. Let her have her movie-night junk food and her probably-free-coffee to go (does anyone think Luke charges Lorelai for coffee?). The woman has been supporting her little family, all on her own, since she was sixteen years old. Giving up movie-night junk food will only make her world bleak and joyless. It will never pay that kind of tuition bill.

But Emily and Richard Gilmore will. A safety net is a beautiful thing. Lorelai spends like

a rich girl, even when her bank account is empty.

The one fancy school in our town is impossible to miss. Let's call it Southern Academy. It sits on the main street running north and south. Beautiful brick buildings and tended green lawns rise on one side of College Road, while athletic fields roll along the other. It's a shiny thing to behold, and before I had a student there, I indeed beheld it longingly. Tuition was prohibitive but they had merit scholarships for their entrance exam's four top-scoring students. H was good at standardized tests. Her beloved elementary school only went through fifth grade. What was the harm in signing her up to take the test, just to see what happened?

Stars Hollow may not exist in this world, but touring Southern Academy, you could believe Chilton might. H was very much a Rory—bright, ambitious, and well behaved. It was impossible for her not to long to be among what seemed like the chosen few at this sparkling school. When she didn't qualify for a scholarship, we dutifully toured other possibilities. We went to parents' night at our neighborhood's public school, we looked at Catholic schools, we applied to charter schools. We applied to the Quaker school where H had attended summer camps, and whose price tag was only marginally higher than her elementary school's.

Our misgivings about Southern Academy weren't just financial. Visit private schools south of the Mason-Dixon Line and you are likely to see a sign out front: Established 1966 or '67. Southern Academy was no different. The administration promised the school had come a long way since its white-flight origins, but to the naked eye this was not visible. The school was not only almost entirely white, but predominantly blond.

David and I discussed this, we did, and worried about it. Shiny things have tarnished edges. But H desperately wanted to go to Southern Academy. We believe in education more than we believe in anything in the world, and we equated the veneer of Southern Academy's buildings and grounds as reflective of the best that could be offered. Most of all, we couldn't bear not to give our child what our parents had given us.

H went to Southern Academy for three years. While not on the level of Choate Rosemary Hall, those three years cost us a grand total of $51,000.

That's a lot of coats.

In season 2 of *Gilmore Girls*, the first few episodes take place in spring and summer. Lorelai does not wear a single coat. When the weather cools, we see her trot out some favorites from the previous year. Good job, wardrobe department, that is some verisimilitude. One does not retire a good leather jacket. Maybe Lorelai has been collecting them for years.

The house where David and I raised our daughter is furnished mostly with Craig's List finds, punctuated by an inherited antique or oil painting. Although Lorelai and Emily are not close enough in size for those coats to be hand-me-downs, several of them might have been Christmas gifts. Lots of modest homes are filled with relics from more prosperous generations.

As season 2 Lorelai heads into winter, we see the return of the fleece-lined jean jacket and the blue puffer, plus some overcoats that may or may not be debuts. Definitely new are the black bouclé coat with metal buttons, a pale gray wool overcoat, a burgundy fleece-lined corduroy jacket, a black sateen overcoat with red and pink roses, and a pink suede jacket.

H phoned while I was writing this. I read her my list of coats and she said, "That makes me want to go thrifting."

Maybe Lorelai buys her coats at thrift shops. Stars Hollow must have a good one. Or maybe millionaires leave them behind in the closets of the Independence Inn.

Or maybe Lorelai just buys them. Maybe she puts them on credit cards. Maybe she sees that pink suede jacket in the window of some perfect store on a perfect street of her perfect town and tries it on and sees that it looks perfect on her. Is she supposed to wait until Richard and Emily die and leave their fortune to her before she owns a beautiful suede jacket? Lorelai grew up in a world where wanting a material thing meant having it. That's a hard world to let go of, even if you recognize the lack of emotional fulfillment it brings. Hopefully the suede jacket is on sale, so she buys it with the last gasps of her paycheck. Later, when the foundation of her house has been eaten by termites, there's no money left. When bank after bank turns Lorelai down, Luke offers to loan her the $15,000. In the end she gets her mother to cosign a bank loan.

We know Carrie Bradshaw's shoe habit got her into financial trouble. But we never hear anyone tell Lorelai Gilmore, Hey. Go a little easier on the coats.

H didn't leave Southern Academy because of money. She put an end to her time there for well-articulated reasons of her own. She transferred to a public school where she thrived for four years, and got into the college of her dreams. Private school used to be a pipeline to the most competitive colleges. I don't believe that's the case anymore. The year H graduated from high school, her public school's roster of university acceptances was equally if not more impressive Southern Academy's.

I used to call the price of lottery tickets a stupidity tax, but now I reserve that phrase for

private school tuition.

Our old friend Mark subsists on so little money, I've urged him to write a book and call it "The Frugal Man's Guide to

Life." Mark reminds me a lot of Luke. He's a coupon-clipper, with no wife or children. He scoffs at the idea of eating at a restaurant. He owns a thick winter coat, a raincoat, and a couple of hoodies.

Luke lives in utilitarian barracks above the diner he inherited from his dad. He dresses in a simple uniform that doesn't vary over the seven seasons of *Gilmore Girls*: flannel shirts, backwards baseball cap, barn jackets. Owning Luke's diner makes takeout a moot point. He doesn't travel. Of course he has $15,000 to offer Lorelai.

Takeout. Tuition. Coats. Children. They can sop up the dregs of any emergency fund.

There's no room to keep listing coats. The best ones show up when Lorelai is out of work, between the Independence and the Dragonfly Inns. I could wax rhapsodic over Lorelai's pink wool overcoat. And the double-breasted black wool coat, she wears it with a matching beanie, and a winning assortment of scarves.

We inherit names. We inherit material things. We inherit attitudes, and places to live. I hold out that Monica Geller's Manhattan apartment in *Friends* is entirely realistic as she took over her grandmother's rent-controlled lease, an opportunity I had—but turned down—when one of my uncles died.

We inherit ideas about what's affordable regardless of the numbers in our ledgers. I can only imagine the ways H will waste money, thanks to the example we've set for her. Early indications are, her extravagance will involve clothing.

As a teenager Lorelai wanted to keep her baby. She wanted

to escape the trappings of excessive wealth. But over the seven seasons of *Gilmore Girls*, wealth calls back to her again and again. She tries to resist. Be good in this life and you'll be rewarded in the hereafter. Forgo the latte and one day you can use that money for something more important, more substantial.

Repair the soles of your shoes instead of buying new ones, make one coat last for five long winters. Invest and save and hope a market correction or crash never makes the joy you lived without disappear into thin air.

Lorelai's coat collection lives not in a front hall closet, but on a wardrobe department's rolling clothes rack—just as Stars Hollow isn't in Connecticut, but on a studio lot called "Midwest Street" in Burbank, California.

I still live in the South. I don't need many coats. My collection is modest. The two best ones are a camel hair coat inherited from a distant relative, and a quilted winter coat with wool sleeves that was a Christmas gift from my mother.

My daughter has two more years of college to go. She chose an expensive one. It's the best money I've ever spent. I will always dream of living in Stars Hollow. I believe Lorelai should go ahead and buy the coats, no matter how the world may tsk. She works hard. They look great on her.

We live once, and it's cold outside.

My Connecticut

Erin Almond

When I mention I'm from Connecticut, I can sometimes tell by people's expressions the Connecticut they envision. It's the one depicted so well in *Gilmore Girls*: quaint villages filled with historic inns and antique shops, suburbs with imposing mansions set amidst professionally manicured lawns. If prep schools and debutante balls aren't your thing, you can always hang out at quirky town halls or toss snowballs in front of the gazebo on the village green. I'm not complaining about this vision—not at all.

The producers of *Gilmore Girls* couldn't have known it at the time, but the show they crafted for seven glorious seasons was the perfect TV fantasy for someone like me. It's as though they took the most difficult parts of my life—leaving home at sixteen, struggling to support myself while working low-wage jobs, making the leap from public school to an elite institution—and placed them in a perfect Connecticut snow globe. Shake it up, and those events become funny, bracing, even heartwarming. When the snow settles, all conflicts are happily resolved. Magic.

To understand why I'm so addicted to *Gilmore Girls*, and why, over the past few years, I've gotten my teenage daughter Josie hooked too, I should tell you about where I grew up, the place I often think of as the "other" Connecticut.

My hometown, East Hartford, was a factory town, its largest employer the aircraft engine manufacturer Pratt & Whitney. When I was a little kid, it was impossible to drive down Main Street when the whistle blew at 5 p.m.; the traffic seemed to back up for miles. Then the layoffs came; the traffic got better, the town got worse. By the early nineties, Main Street was a cemetery of empty storefronts, rent-by-the-hour motels, and adult bookstores. The surrounding streets were filled with dingy apartments and low-slung ranch homes. Picture the basement of one of those houses, inside of which was a band room that contained a tiger-striped drum set, a Peavey guitar amp, and a red velvet love seat whose cushions hid the moldering remains of discarded Pringles.

Two teenage girls sat in that room—one behind the drum set, one on the couch with an electric guitar on her lap—smoking Camel Lights while taking a break from playing Mötley Crüe's *Shout at the Devil*. They sipped cheap beer and talked about how they were going to be rock stars someday. The girl behind the drums was nicknamed Duckie. The girl on the couch was me, a sixteen-year-old runaway who couldn't quite believe she'd made it out of her parents' house, where guitars, cigarettes, and of course beer were all banned.

As any *Gilmore Girls* fan knows, Lorelai Gilmore also left home at sixteen. There's no doubt my obsession arises from this parallel: the need to break away from a controlling mother. But the similarities pretty much end there.

Lorelai flees the mansion she grew up in after refusing to marry the teenage father of her child. In fact, Lorelai has been chafing against her mother's expectations for most her life: formal dinners, debutante balls and "coming-out" parties, a narrow, snobbish view of life. In the *Gilmore Girls* snow globe, this conflict takes the form of lighthearted banter and inside jokes. (No wonder Lorelai loves eating Pop-Tarts and marshmallows covered in chocolate sauce, given the stilted, formal meals she suffered through as a child!)

Maternal control looked very different in my Connecticut. Mom, a devout Catholic, smashed my *Shout at the Devil* tape with a hammer in our backyard. She also grounded me for most of my ninth-grade year, for infractions ranging from benign (wearing tight jeans) to dire (sneaking out of the house at night). When the groundings no longer seemed sufficient, my parents brought back corporal punishment—not the spankings of childhood but actual beatings.

One afternoon, my mother grounded me for saying "damn." I repeated the offensive word and she added another week. I stormed upstairs, slammed my door, and blasted Metallica.

She burst into my room and told me she was taking away my stereo, too. She tried to slap me, I blocked her. We shoved and punched each other, and Mom grabbed a handful of my hair and pulled as hard as she could. Later, gingerly rubbing my head, I retrieved a clump pulled out by the roots. I ran down the street to a friend's house. Her mom called the police. When questioned, my mother claimed I'd cut the hair off a doll in order to "frame" her.

I began scouring apartment listings, looking for a room I could afford on the $5.50 an hour I made working behind the counter at Riccardo's Music Center. I was walking down Maple Street, working up the courage to knock on the door of one of those places, when Duckie drove by in her rust-colored Grenada. When I told her what I was up to, she lit a Camel Light, using the tip of the one she was already smoking, and handed it to me. I was moving into her basement, she told me. She was sure her mother wouldn't mind.

When Lorelai Gilmore leaves home, baby in tow, she moves to Stars Hollow, works as a maid at the Independence Inn, and lives in the potting shed out back. Not much time is spent showing viewers exactly how this arrangement worked when Rory was a toddler. By the time we meet Lorelai in the pilot, Rory is sixteen, and appears to be the functioning adult in that relationship. Lorelai loves junk food, is impulsive and funny. Rory is a straight-A student recently accepted to Chilton, an elite prep school.

This, of course, is the setup that compels Lorelai to get back in touch with her parents, Richard and Emily, because the only way for her to afford Chilton's steep tuition is to ask for their help. The elder Gilmores agree, with one stipulation: Lorelai and Rory must attend Friday night dinners each week at their Hartford mansion. Undoubtedly, Richard and Emily actually lived in West Hartford, across the Connecticut River from homely East Hartford. In my teens, Hartford was where you went to sneak into clubs with a fake ID. Later, it was the city I drove through to get to the wealthy towns on the other side—towns where a young woman could work in restaurants that catered to upscale clientele, and thus earn excellent tips.

It was obvious by then, two years after I'd moved into Duckie's basement, that the whole rock-star thing wasn't working out for me. My friend Beth, who grew up west of the river, was the one who suggested I apply for a job working with her at a fancy Italian restaurant in Avon. Curious, I met her there for dinner one night, to take advantage of her employee discount. I'd imagined pepperoni pizza, pasta with red sauce, and garlic bread.

Instead, on the embossed menu, I encountered words such as *portobello*, *calamari*, and *prosciutto*, which Beth had to translate. I cautiously made my way through the dishes when they arrived, suddenly conscious of a palate accustomed to tuna on white bread and Quarter Pounders with cheese.

I don't remember which dishes I liked, but I do remember one of the managers delivering our fried calamari. The plate accidentally tipped, and some of the calamari spilled onto my seat. "Oh no!" I gasped, picking up the rings and putting them back on the plate. Beth and the manager laughed. He made a joke about the daily special being "Banquette Calamari." My face burned. I was sure I'd revealed something shameful about myself, how much I'd had to scrounge to pay for even the discounted version of that meal.

Once hired, I got regular glimpses of the Connecticut the Gilmores represent. I served women in fur coats, men who bragged about their golf scores, and the Ivy League tuitions of their children. I once overheard a woman at the bar lamenting to a friend—over snifters of Grey Goose—that her children had asked for the nanny when she'd tried to tuck them in. I hadn't known any families who employed nannies growing up; my parents barely ever hired a babysitter.

But it wasn't until the restaurant owners opened another location in Glastonbury—the rural town that bordered East Hartford—that I truly understood the lines dividing my Connecticut from the Gilmores' version. When the owner's wife offered to show the new bistro to a friend, the friend demurred. "I never cross the river," she said, raising a snifter to her lips, "not even to go to Glastonbury."

It will come as no surprise that one of the most seductive aspects of *Gilmore Girls*, to me, is the ease with which Lorelai and Rory shuttle between these two Connecticuts. In any given episode you might see Lorelai happily overdosing on French fries and coffee at Luke's diner, then handing her coat to the maid at her parents' mansion; Rory walking the hallowed halls of Yale University, then wolfing takeout from Al's Pancake World.

This class mobility extends to their dating lives, too: Lorelai has many suitors across the seven seasons, but the ones who recur most often are Rory's father, Christopher, who announces in the show's penultimate season that he's inherited so much money from his grandfather he'd like to buy Rory a castle, and, of course, Luke, the baseball-cap-wearing local who has held the keys to Lorelai's heart since the show's first episode.

It's notable that none of the locales featured in *Gilmore Girls*, neither Stars Hollow nor Richard and Emily's Hartford, look anything like East Hartford. Nor do any of the episodes show what it's really like to leave your family as a teenager and work low-wage jobs. You never see Lorelai walking into a grocery store with a ten-dollar bill, calculating what she might buy with it that could feed her for a week, or figuring out how much more debt she can add to her trio of maxed-out credit cards when her car breaks down.

Although we only ever see it in brief flashbacks, we do know that Lorelai was looked after by the owner of the Independence Inn—an ebullient woman named Mia, whom Emily Gilmore clearly envies—and it's implied that Mia's support was key to Lorelai working her way

up through the inn's ranks.

As a teen runaway, I had my own version of Mia watching over me: Duckie's mother, Kathy. My mom was probably envious of Kathy, too, although that only occurs to me now, thirty years later. Maybe that's why, on the day I left home, as Duckie helped lug my stuff out to her car, my mom called Kathy and told her I was a drug addict and that she would regret taking me in. Duckie's mom said it sounded like time apart would be good for us; she figured I'd be staying only for a couple of weeks.

Three years later, I moved out of Duckie's basement and into a crappy apartment in East Hartford's North End. I worked as many jobs as I could to make my rent and stay one payment ahead of my credit card bills. I delivered pizza and bartended in New Britain at a venue where the employees were encouraged to drink alongside the patrons. I sometimes went out on dates with guys I wasn't attracted to because I knew I'd get a free meal, and I spent a month cocktail waitressing at a strip club near the state university because, again, good tips.

Still, there were times when I was so hungry and exhausted that I just sat on my bed and cried. No matter how hard I worked, my debt grew deeper. I bought lottery tickets and practiced my instruments and dreamed, but getting out of East Hartford felt more impossible than ever.

In the snow globe, Lorelai works her way up to manager at the Independence Inn with enough of a financial cushion to purchase her own home, not to mention the copious candy and takeout meals she and Rory consume, to comic effect, each week. When the series begins, she's taking business classes at night—not urgently, out of economic need, but because she dreams of opening her own inn.

In my Connecticut, night school—community college— saved my life. After earning an associate's degree, I received a scholarship to finish my bachelor's at Wesleyan. And once I began clawing my way up from near poverty to a potential member of the middle class, I increasingly felt like I belonged nowhere. I was awed by the assurance of most Wesleyan students, the ease with which they argued with our professors, or protested decisions made by the administration, while I walked around with the constant suspicion that someone was going to figure out I'd been admitted by mistake. When I visited East Hartford, the dive bars where I'd once partied now seemed depressing. "You don't dress like a slut anymore," an old friend observed, disapprovingly.

There is something I had in common with Lorelai and Rory, though: I couldn't apply to Wesleyan on my own. Even with my scholarship, I needed my parents to fill out their income information to qualify for federal grants and loans. That meant returning to the house I'd left in a puff of cigarette smoke and rage—my father yelling from the kitchen table, "Don't let the door hit your ass on the way out!"—to ask for their help.

Dad was the easy one, actually. He was the person who'd recommended I attend community college, and after seeing me walking to one of my jobs, signed the permission slip that allowed me to get my driver's license at seventeen. Their attitude toward my ambitions was one of profound ambivalence. On the one hand, they grumbled that I shouldn't get "too big for my britches." On the other, they were proud that I'd gotten into Wesleyan, a school they knew only by reputation. I would be the first person to earn a bachelor's degree in our family. In the end, they filled out and signed the forms.

Once I was at Wesleyan, Dad occasionally slipped me a hundred-dollar bill, out of sight of Mom, during my visits home. Maybe he understood there was no way I could hold my own, financially, with kids who flew off to London during winter break, or whose CEO fathers offered to take their daughter's housemates out to a four-star restaurant. He wanted me to know that he could still help me out, even though I thought I was doing all that clawing for myself. In *Gilmore Girls*, Rory is the one who makes the leap from public high school to elite prep school, and finally to Yale. But she's not breaking new ground—in fact, she's returning to the class her mother rejected. One of the reasons Rory decides to attend Yale, even though she's dreamed of Harvard her entire life, is that her grandfather is an alum.

It also becomes clear, in the snow globe, that the economic contract between Lorelai and Rory, and Emily and Richard, is a façade—the excuse for the characters to avoid talking about what happened when Lorelai discovered she was pregnant with Rory all those years ago. Instead of apologizing, Richard and Emily agree to pay Rory's Chilton fees and then her Yale tuition—as long as she and Lorelai continue to show up for weekly dinners.

This is why Emily gets so upset when Christopher comes into his inheritance and decides that, as Rory's father, he should pay for Yale. Emily is sure that means the end of regular visits with her daughter and granddaughter, although Lorelai assures her that's not the case. "Without your money, Rory would have graduated from Stars Hollow High and gone to community college," Lorelai tells her mother.

This line has always measured the distance between Lorelai's Connecticut and my own. But I, too, had an implicit contract with my parents. They helped out with my Wesleyan tuition, and provided me a place to stay after graduation. Even after I rented an apartment closer to my new job at a software company in Stamford, I still returned to East Hartford most weekends. I'd visit my parents for our version of Friday night dinner and then go hang out with my musician friends. I'd trade my business casual for ripped jeans and crop tops, sometimes even pick up my guitar. I wanted to inhabit both Connecticuts, I suppose, and for a time that seemed possible.

But the contract between me and my parents didn't hold. As the years went by, it was harder for me to remain silent about what happened when I was a teen: the groundings and beatings, the letter my mother wrote attempting to get me expelled from the alternative high school program that enabled me to attend school while also working. When I tried to talk about those things, my father left the room, while my mother seemed panicked and claimed that I, her child, had abused her.

It is this bitter form of combat—shame and resentment exploding into arguments that escalate into estrangement—that I most lament when it comes to my Connecticut. And it's what makes me such a sucker for the *Gilmore* version.

My favorite episode of the entire series is "Friday Night's Alright for Fighting." A fight breaks out during Friday night dinner, and Rory and her grandparents threaten to leave. But Lorelai convinces them to stay put: "Now, we all agreed to have Friday night dinner, and we're here, and I smell dinner. And yes, apparently there are some issues to be worked out, but no one, and I mean no one, is leaving here until we do!"

What follows is a surreal mash-up of invective, laughter, and banal conversation that, for me, is the ultimate Connecticut fantasy: the ability to air every grievance and emerge a stronger family for it. When the night is done, and Lorelai and Rory step back outside—their hair mussed and their scarves askew—viewers understand that snow globe has been mightily shaken. "Well, I think we've officially reinstated Friday night dinner," Lorelai declares.

That's the kind of relationship I want to have with my own teenage daughter—all my kids, really. I don't control the music Josie listens to, or the clothes she wears. I have never, and would never, hit her. She confides in me about what's going on in her life, and I'm in awe of what she's already accomplished at seventeen—the age I was when I was living in Duckie's basement—as a climate activist, amateur historian, and published writer.

While I no longer bring her back to my Connecticut, I'm grateful we can watch *Gilmore Girls* together. It's fun to visit the snow globe, to spend time with a fictional family devoted to each other despite their differences, who meet each week over martinis at a comically large house in Hartford. When the show is over, Josie and I gather with the rest of our family around our own dinner table, where none of the plates match and there is no maid or cook, but the conversation is honest, the food homemade, and each person seen and loved for who they truly are.

A Place to Stay

Francesco Sedita

I watched season 1 of *Gilmore Girls*, like any red-blooded American should have, when it first aired in 2000. At the time, I worked for an upstart internet promotions company (I still don't really know what we did) and was surrounded by creative people, mostly about my age, who adored the show. And while the other men in the group often went out during lunchtime, I became part of the *Gilmore Girls* lunchtime talk, about Sookie, about coffee, about Lorelai's coats. About Friday night dinners at Emily Gilmore's house. About Luke. Luke! But even with the handsome parade of beaus, the one thing I focused on, much to the chagrin of my cohorts, was Lorelai's house. I wanted to snuggle on that gloriously comfortable couch, watching VHS movies, passing popcorn back and forth, while Lorelai told stories of loves once lost and Rory helped us both understand the shape of the world, speaking in simple terms, making it all sound so easy.

When the company closed, as all internet companies did at that time, I lost touch with Lorelai and Rory. Instead, I fell in love with Sydney Bristow, with *24*, with *Survivor*. And never checked in on my friends in Stars Hollow. And then 2020 happened, and while I was trapped in my apartment, when my husband went to bed, I took the journey back there and felt comforted in a way that was quite difficult to achieve that year. Lorelai's house, with all its creaks and quirks, seemed even more appealing. What would it be like to stay there?

My family has a long history with homes and places to live. I was born on Mott Street, Little Italy, New York City. My mother grew up in the same building. After she married my dad, they moved into apartment 4G—one floor below my mother's childhood apartment. That was 1963. The year President Kennedy was assassinated. The year a vaccine for measles was approved. When Martin Luther King had a dream. When Jim Whittaker climbed Mount Everest. The Beatles were about to become *the* Beatles. And my mother said, "I do."

This five-story building, with a tarred roof that served as sanctuary to my uncle's pigeons, its official address 55 East Houston Street, also served as home to countless family members. Aunts, uncles, great-aunts and great-uncles, cousins, grandparents, and people the family decided to adopt— including the queer man on the fourth floor who dressed in drag, and whom my father and Uncle Ronny physically defended many times over the years—lined the hallways of the building.

But when I was born, in 1974, 4G, a one-bedroom with steam heat, became too small too quickly, especially because my sister lived there, too. Six years older than I, Danielle has memories of 4G that I just don't. And even more than that, in the years pre-me, my sister lived with my parents in Mexico City and Honolulu. They moved to those locations not for vacation but to set up businesses: women's health clubs before the days of Jack LaLanne and Lucille Roberts.

Mott Street, Little Italy, in New York City in 1974 looked nothing like it does now. NoLita, it's called today, with its sushi restaurants and well-appointed bridal shops and clunky cafés. Places where you wait twenty-five minutes for a twenty-six-dollar avocado toast and an eighteen-dollar Negroni. It's a place of beautiful street art, of families with double-wide strollers, of clothing and jewelry fairs. As it was then, this is all centered around St. Patrick's Old Cathedral, where we were baptized, where my parents were married, and where I was allowed to roam the dark catacombs under the church because my grandfather "had a key." Where too many funerals of too many good people (and lots of terrible people) were held. There's more to say here. Before NoLita, Mott Street was a place for the Mafia. The real deal. Pistols in suit jackets, baseball bats behind counters. Crime. Drugs. Murders. Secrets and affairs.

Wanting to take the family away from that, wanting more space and a new start, my parents moved us to Randolph, New Jersey. The sticks. Born and raised near Hell's Kitchen, my father loved New Jersey—the enormous front and back yards, where he could have a garden, like his father might have had in Sicily. I don't know what my mother thought, really. She was so close to her family and it must have been torturous to leave them. But she had to have felt relief, too, to get away from the messier parts. They bought an acre of land with a new house on it, four bedrooms, three bathrooms, a two-car garage, an eat-in kitchen where countless pots of gravy were to be cooked, and a basement that they'd finish in wall-to-wall blue shag carpet, and which became the main office for their work: Danielle Bari Figure Salons. All for $75,000. Paid for, partly, in the cash they'd saved in a secret shoebox. Before this, my mother worked on Wall Street and my father owned and ran a hair salon on 34th Street. The story goes that the Pan Am girls couldn't get enough of him.

My mother designed this house. An elevated formal dining room and living room, with a half-circle, soft white couch, one we weren't allowed to sit on. A table before it, a thick, round slab of glass atop six thick green blocks. The drapes, depending on the season, were either chocolate brown or pale beige. A man with a ladder changed them as temperatures changed. Carpeted walls, leather couches in the family room, a playroom for us, a music room for my dad's records. This house was chic. Not fancy or grand or fussy, like Emily and Richard Gilmore's house. Chic.

My bedroom, with creamy blue walls and windows that cranked open onto the front lawn, allowing in the glow of the Christmas lights in the cold and the scent of the weeping cherry trees in the warm, became my sanctuary. All in one place, I had my stuffed animals, a small TV, and a stereo, where I listened to music like *Free to Be . . . You and Me*, and later, Madonna.

This is the room where my grandfather taught me how to tell time on a Snoopy clock that started its ring by saying "Hey, Snoopy! I know you're allergic to mornings . . ." The room where my pet hamster, coincidentally also named Snoopy, fell off the bed in a plastic hamster ball. I thought he was going to die and didn't sleep for two nights, worrying. Where I hatched a butterfly. Where I got caught dancing to Prince, naked, swinging my towel around. Where I programmed countless hours of code into a computer plugged into my TV in order to play a singular game of checkers.

And which disappeared forever when I finally turned my TV off.

My sister had the room next to mine and all of the things a young teenager was supposed to have in the 1980s. Puffy rainbows on the walls, a four-poster red wood bed and matching furniture. Red! An antique vanity, lined with her shimmering lip glosses and kohl eyeliners, her powders and foundations, mousses and sprays. And one day, red-pinned above that vanity, the *Purple Rain* record sleeve, the lyrics to "Darling Nikki" in plain sight. And then.

And then, in the summer of 1985, my parents sat us down, telling us we had to move. That we had to leave this house, the only one I knew. The house I would run laps around to burn energy, with a garden I worked in with my dad. The house that got so many trick-or-treaters, we kept a tally. The house where my father dressed as Santa.

They were bankrupt. It was time to find our potting shed at the Independence Inn. We moved to a small rental after doing two garage sales, when we sold as much as possible. A stereo system, the big wooden kitchen table that wouldn't fit in our new house, some of my board games and old stuffies. My mother insisted on keeping the white couch, and so we did. People asked questions and they politely dodged answers.

A woman named Judy from Weichert Realtors became their agent and took great care of my family. She'd been through a terrible fire in her home years before. She understood real pain and recognized it in my parents and became their friend. And sold that house for every penny she could get for them. Judy, who used to do funny accents to make me laugh. Whose Cadillac my father jokingly put a sign in the windshield of at one of the garage sales that read "$750."

But it was my mother who found our next house, not Judy. On one of her drives, to clear her head, still somehow in the powder blue Cadillac, the lights of which went from high to low beam on their own. The house had three bedrooms. Two on the main floor, and the third floor became my parents' bedroom. The house itself was nice, in an old lady kind of way. It possessed a sad energy, mostly from us, but with some of its own. Floors creaked and wind whistled. The off-limits white couch became the couch. A basement lurked below, one with areas slightly too dark and terrifying. It was here that my bunny, Matilda, was killed by a dog in her backyard hutch (this is for another essay, but it must be noted that I only found out that this had been the demise of Matilda, my precious black and white bunny, when I was *forty-five* years old. I'd been told she ran away. Talk about the power of mother-and-daughter bonds).

We lived in that house for two years, as my parents slowly rebuilt their lives. I got a bike and rode around the neighborhood, living closer to many of my friends, and getting invited to sleepovers and birthday parties at Chuck E. Cheese. My sister, who no longer had the Firebird she'd gotten for her sixteenth birthday, drove around with her friend Linda and made out with boys. And our lives just sort of went on.

Then, later, we moved to another home, nearby. Our parents didn't have an Emily or Richard to ask—or not ask—for help. Found on another one of my mother's drives, this house was nicer, the next step toward stabilizing, and my parents were proud. I spent my teen years here with a new addition to the family, a dopey, sweet Siberian husky I named Nanook.

It was here that I acted and sang terribly in shows like *Oklahoma!* and *No, No, Nanette*. Where I called in sick thirty-two times in my first year of high school, an all-boys Catholic prep that offered me a scholarship. This is where my sister had her knee surgeries. The house her friend moved into for a time when she had family hardship. And where my sister and I threw our one and only party together while our parents were away at a family wedding. A party so epic, Morris Plains heartthrob Timothy Rogers showed up on roller skates and glided around our kitchen for hours, drinking Jack Daniel's from the bottle, while I secretly swooned.

And it was from this house that I left for NYU, into the arms of my beloved New York City. And now, where I live in a sunny apartment with my husband Doug, and an orange cat named Alfredo. It's here that we cook Sunday dinners, while we pick at meats and cheeses, just like I did with my family. It's here that we've hosted cramped and delicious Christmases, far too large for our space. And here where we returned from our wedding in 2017, after a weekend of love, happiness, and vow sharing. When I got distance from my homes, as I moved through dorm rooms, roommates, and my place with Doug, I've often wondered: Wasn't I supposed to feel happiest in the dream house my parents created in 1974? Wasn't that the house that was the—what—best? And while I think fondly about my time in that house, I see so clearly now that it was the other homes— where we weren't our best selves, where we often bumped up against one another and the world, the ones where the white couch lost its luster, where we white-knuckled it together, to grow together, to allow all the furniture to be used, to cram the same number of people into those smaller kitchens at holidays.

Those were my homes.

I loved Lorelai's house because it was a home. Because after growing up in Emily and Richard's house, she made a space that would nurture and grow her proudest accomplishment, Rory. And just like my parents, Lorelai Gilmore made sure her child always had a place to rest her weary head and to dream of more.

Hiding in the Floorboards

Sanjena Sathian

There's an iconic moment early in the first season of *Gilmore Girls* when Rory Gilmore swings by her best friend Lane Kim's house to borrow a CD. Lane, a spunky Korean American teen played by Keiko Agena, obliges by lifting up loose floorboards in her room to reveal a massive collection of the secular rock-and-roll albums her religious mother won't allow her to consume.

I was not, myself, actually allowed to consume *Gilmore Girls* either, which has a mildly scandalous premise: it follows Rory and her thirtysomething single mom, Lorelai, who got pregnant as a teenager. Parenthood out of wedlock was not condoned in my Indian immigrant household—or in Lane's. (As Lane tells Lorelai, Mrs. Kim "doesn't trust unmarried women.") Nevertheless, I watched *Gilmore Girls* surreptitiously, and instinctually loved Lane's rebellious hijinks. She contrives elaborate codes and alibis to finagle a single phone call with a boy. She plans a KGB-worthy covert drop to have Rory deliver the new Belle and Sebastian single when she gets grounded for dating. She tries to "come out" to her mother as a rebel a few times—once memorably dyeing her hair purple and then redyeing it black in terror; another time calling Mrs. Kim while drunk and declaring her intoxication.

When I was in graduate school, a white guy once read my fiction and noted that my characters—second-generation South Asian teens growing up in a socially conservative immigrant bubble—engaged in "contained debauchery," as though they should have been a little harder-core. Lane's debauchery might have seemed contained to an outsider, but I know it was plenty serious for her.

In Lane's scheming, I recognize an exaggerated version of the code-switching that some children of immigrants cultivate as a survival strategy, and in Mrs. Kim's unbending responses, I see a familiar portrait of a mother intent on protecting her child from the unholy American trifecta of drinking, drugs, and dating. Like Lane, I loved art, often art the adults in my community disapproved of; like Lane, I sequestered my tastes beneath the proverbial floorboards.

Like Mrs. Kim, who eventually (and heartbreakingly) discovers Lane's secret stash and unravels years of lies—and, hurt and afraid, fears she has lost her daughter—my parents got wise to my various misbehaviors and shoddy cover-ups. And finally, like the Kims, who find a tenuous peace as Lane enters her twenties, my family and I started to learn how our occasionally diverging values can coexist now that I'm an adult.

And yet I had none of this language when I was watching *Gilmore Girls* when it first aired in the early 2000s. As a teenager, I wasn't seeing *myself* in Lane. I didn't even think of myself as "Asian American," except when I had to check a box on a standardized form. Then, I reentered the *Gilmore Girls'* utopian setting of Stars Hollow, Connecticut, in the spring of 2021, coming off a year of anti-Asian sentiment, including the spa shooting that killed eight people, most of them Asian women. Turning to the show for comfort, and watching through my post-vaccine haze, I realized how complex my feelings about Lane are, and how much they mimic the complexities I feel about laying claim to the term "Asian American" at all.

Growing up, I was only Indian—not even "South Asian" (a term I learned in college). And there were probably more material differences than similarities between Lane and me. My parents are Hindu, not Christian like the Kims—Mrs. Kim's rigid Seventh-Day Adventism (based on Korean American *Gilmore Girls* producer Helen Pai's real life) would have been deeply bizarre in my household. My Ivy League-striving, upper-middle-class Indian American bubble resembled Rory's white, posh prep school more than Mrs. Kim's antique store. I went to Yale and became a journalist like Rory. I lived in Rory's freshman dorm (Durfee) and wore those newspaper hats the heelers (aspiring *YDN*ers) don. Lane, on the other hand, doesn't finish college; the one her mother briefly sends her to is a Christian school that bans nail polish and spicy condiments.

Religion and class aside, we simply didn't look alike; we couldn't pass for each other, and wouldn't get mixed up by the carpool moms who often swapped out my name for the other Indian girls'. (Notably, Agena and Emily Kuroda, who plays Mrs. Kim, are Japanese American, not Korean, which suggests the show did conflate East Asians—a practice that was all too common twenty years ago and persists today.) Our parents' languages and family foods were distinct. That both of our roots could be traced to the Eastern half of Eurasia seemed irrelevant, given the size of that landmass. My priority in those years wasn't identifying opportunities for solidarity with other othered people. It was hard enough to articulate who I was just to myself.

My adolescent ambivalence about the unwieldy term "Asian American," which includes Bangladeshis, Bhutanese, Thais, Taiwanese, and everyone in between, is not unique. Many Asian Americans feel unmoved or even angered by the phrase "Asian American," which fails to sum up so many varied cultures. And though my subject matter here is a feel-good dramedy, the inadequacy of the epithet has high stakes and a real history beyond Stars Hollow. The "model minority" narrative of all Asians being like rich, high-achieving Indians, for instance, can shape policy that disenfranchises poorer Asians like Hmong students.

That spring of 2021, when I rewatched *Gilmore Girls* for the umpteenth time and turned my attention to Lane, anxiety over what it meant to be Asian American seemed to be at a peak. Some South Asians felt that those calling to "Stop AAPI Hate" in the wake of attacks on East Asians didn't tap into the same rage when four Sikh workers were murdered at an Indianapolis FedEx. South Asians have a particularly baffling racial history of being classified, at various intervals, as Black, Caucasian, Asian, and none of the above.

Personally, I experience a kind of vertigo about "Asian America." I've boned up on the AAPI history, contributed to the AAPI reading lists, penned the AAPI think pieces, and written an AAPI novel, and yet sometimes, all the talk about the label makes me feel like I'm just spinning on the spot, getting nowhere new, only making myself sick.

When, while feverish from Pfizer dose two, I switched on *Gilmore Girls*, I did not plan on thinking about the ways "Asian America" functions for me. I was *already* sick. I had absconded into Stars Hollow for the comfort it provides, not to analyze it. But the landscape of the show looked different fifteen years after I first saw it. I grasped, suddenly, that I don't share anything inherent with Lane. Some might see in both of our stories something essentially "Asian"—the apocryphal "tiger parents," a desire to assimilate. But these aren't, of course, racial qualities. They're social. What I share with Lane isn't Eastern roots—it's the self-consciousness with which we must react, respond, and relate to America, as outsiders to this country.

The Kims and the Sathians defined parts of ourselves in

rejoinder to mainstream white America, which makes for a comic pendulum: adults ban rock music or TV shows that acknowledge premarital sex; kids seek out the contraband. This feels like a synecdoche of the way Asian American identity has been formed—reactively. Though the term "Asian American" was originated by 1960s radical left-wing students building a "coalition" of identities (as the poet Cathy Park Hong has put it) to resist imperialism and capitalism, Asians were lumped together before we united together. Racist American policies have intermittently banned migration from Asia for a century and a half and continue to cast Asians as perpetual foreigners or traitors (see: Manzanar; Guantánamo Bay; COVID-related attacks).

It can sometimes feel like we've been legislated or sociologized into an identity rather than adopting it ourselves, which might be why Lane—and I—got so serious about artistic self-invention. But after all that, we're often still marginal. This dynamic even played out within *Gilmore Girls* itself—Lane was always the B-plot to the white people's A-plots, and fan consensus is that her arc tanked as the show progressed into Rory's WASPy Yale world.

Often, the contemporary discourse of representation suggests that the point of putting minorities on-screen is to provoke something like a second mirror stage. In seeing someone who "looks like us" on television or in film, our identities are theoretically validated. But so much of what's interesting about relating to other people happens in the space between what we recognize and what we do not. And perhaps this is one way of thinking about Asian Americanness—that the work and joy of it occur in that weave and bob, in the movement between being crowded together and choosing to crowd together. But then again, maybe I just need to justify the many hours I've spent with my head in Stars Hollow.

Daughter Is a Permanent State

Yassmin Abdel-Magied

> One need never become a mother.
> But to have a mother is to be finite.
> To say "my mother" is to be mortal.
>
> —*Eugenie Brinkema*

I was introduced to the *Gilmore Girls* by my half-Haitian Mormon friend on a warm Christmas day in a rural Australian town. This was my first-ever "real" Christmas; growing up in a Sudanese Muslim family, the twenty-fifth of December was remarkable only for its ability to shut the doors of our local McDonald's. My friend, the other Black person at the Youth Parliament camp I attended that winter break, had invited me to share the festive period with her family. Beset by curiosity and the wayward sense of adventure that characterised my late teens, I agreed.

My own family had little idea I was making this pilgrimage. All they knew was I was working a vacation job in a coal mine nine hours' drive north of my hometown, Brisbane. It was 2008. In my state, coal jobs were the best jobs—the only jobs—for engineering students like me: hungry, ambitious, skint. The summer placement would cover my expenses for an entire year, and this promise of financial freedom, garnished with the argument it was "good for my CV," was enough to convince my parents to let their seventeen-year-old hijabi daughter, who had never spent more than a few days away from home, move five hundred miles away to work coal. Parental permission secured, I informed my team at Youth Without Borders, the grassroots organisation I'd founded a year earlier, and the board of the Queensland Museum I had just joined, that I'd be out of town for a few months. I peppered my emails with text-based emojis, unable to hide my excitement. I would be working. How utterly grown up! I was grown up, my mother reminded me. I was a professional. An adult woman, and the men in the mine would treat me as such. My mother's advice was delivered in a single kitchen-bench conversation, the night before I set off. Her care was packaged in typical bluntness, as if I were being read my rights over tea.

Don't wear tight trousers. Never let a man into your room. Only read educational nonfiction, leave that fantasy, childish stuff behind. Don't be a show-off, but remember to show your leadership skills. Don't talk about yourself all the time. I am proud of you. Well done.

My mother confused me. In some ways, I was her mirror image. We had the same off-the-wall sense of humour, cared about the same causes, and looked so much alike that when we travelled back to Sudan, my aunts would mistake me for their sister. She was also my biggest believer. I would not have had the courage to start Youth Without Borders had it not been for her encouraging question: "If you want to, why not?"

But my mother's belief came with sky-high expectations, floating out of reach anytime I got close enough to touch. I found it unbearable, and she seemed unable to understand why. Mama only wanted what was best for me, didn't I see that? Was that not a mother's job? So, unlike Rory, the daughter in the show I was soon to become obsessed with, my life was not an open book. I shared scant details of my ever-evolving life with my mother, not out of fear of a fire-and-brimstone-style punishment, but out of a sapling's barely conscious desire to bask in the warmth of a higher power. I wanted to be—or be seen as—good, in the eyes of my parents and in the eyes of my God, which at that point was all but the same thing. I wanted to meet those atmospheric standards, be "good enough," be the perfect daughter.

Rory was clever, witty, and knew her own mind. She ate her body weight in junk food, cared little for what others thought of her, was at ease with her ambitions and achieved them effort-lessly. Most importantly, Rory was more than good enough for her mother. In Lorelai's eyes, Rory could do no wrong. She was the perfect daughter. But Brisbane was no Stars Hollow, and my mother had far more in common with Emily Gilmore than with Lorelai.

I spent much of my adolescence and young adulthood desperate to be bathed in the light of my mother's approval, committed to the asymptotic pursuit. But every so often the embers of adventure would tempt me away from the pure light of her sun. My leaves would turn, compelled by tropism towards the open skies of the unknown. I knew a "good" Sudanese girl didn't take three Greyhound buses by herself across the country to spend a week with a family her parents hadn't vetted and approved. I knew a "good" Sudanese girl would call her parents every night, diligently reporting who she had met and what she had done. I knew a "good" Sudanese girl didn't take a job in another town unless she was married, but that ship had long since sailed.

While I was on my way to defining my own sense of being a Sudanese girl, I was holding on to the fiction that I could be both: what my mother wanted me to be and what I chose. The desire to break free, and the seeming impossibility of it. Where did that leave me? Somehow, in the safe and wholesome world of the *Gilmore Girls*, I found characters grappling with similar questions.

At the time I visited in the late 2000s, Dalby, the land of the Baranggum First Nations People, was a town of under ten thousand inhabitants. According to the *Gilmore Girls* fandom wiki, that places the rural centre at roughly the same size as

Stars Hollow. An agricultural hub, Dalby is well known for being the centre of a rich grain and cotton growing industry. It is far less known for its racial diversity. On arrival, we joked I had increased the Black population by 20 percent. Again, not too unlike Stars Hollow.

The journey to my friend's place was fractious and confusing, featuring a missed bus connection, an awkward hostel stay in a twelve-bed room, a seven-hour wait on Christmas morning at another bus depot, and a nervousness that somehow, I was going to be caught out. But I made it, eventually, to the hot sweep of the Darling Downs, with its ochre fertile soil and verdant rolling hills.

My friend's home was a gorgeous two-storey house set back behind a forest of eucalypts, standing guard like sentries. I don't remember seeing any koalas on that trip, but I probably did, their grey fur camouflaged among the branches of dappled grey and white, laconic and drowsy. Queensland's heat will do that to you, the baking heat rising from the earth slowing you down like molasses, nudging you towards shade, stillness, cool. They had the tree, and the lights, and the food, and the crackers, and everything I imagined to expect from watching Love Actually. But my ignorance was on full display. I worried my tardiness meant I had missed the religious portion of the festivities, only to learn that Mormons did not attend Christmas mass at all, the focus of the day being on family and togetherness. My lack of preparedness bit me at every turn: embarrassingly, I had not considered needing to bring a present for each member of the family, whereas they had all thought of me in their gift giving. My reasoning for keeping the Dalby adventure from my parents would soon morph from worry about their disapproval into shame at being such a poor houseguest. We trained you far better than this, my mother would scold, and she would be right. But my hosts were generous, kind and gracious, welcoming my haphazard presence as its own blessing.

And soon, in the cosy hours between Christmas lunch and Christmas dinner, when bellies are full and conversation slackens, my friend drew me into her room, patted a flat spot in the mess of her duvet, and invited me into a new universe. We were only meant to watch the first episode, maybe the second. In the end, we had dinner in bed, balancing plates on our knees, the room darkening around us, our faces lit up by the flickering of the small TV. I don't remember what time we went to sleep that night, I'm not sure I ever did. I kept wanting more, more, more of this world. They had so much to say, and it was all so funny, and genuine, and nice? The Gilmore dynamics felt familiar and foreign, all at once. I inhaled the show like I was taking my first full breath.

I had no template for the world of the *Gilmore Girls*. I knew nobody who was friends with their mother the way Rory was with Lorelai, had no conception of an adult who did not act like what I understood an adult to be. Here was a grown woman with a grown child whose relationship with her own mother still resembled my own. "Rory and I are best friends, Mom. We're best friends first and mother and daughter second," says Lorelai to Emily in episode 16 of the second season, an admission so profound it threatened to breach my blood-brain barrier. What did that even mean? Wasn't that unnatural? Yet I watched on, unable to tell whether this was something I wanted, or decried, or both.

In the subsequent decade or so since the show aired (I do not consider the Netflix Original *A Year in the Life* to be a valid part of the canon, we can argue about that in another anthology), I have pondered over what drew me in so securely to the world of the three generations of Gilmore girls.

In 2016, *Vox* published a piece positing that the show's popularity had something to do with its politics. "Running for almost the entirety of the Bush years, the show was an antidote to the conservative values that pervaded that era," author Noah Gittell observed under the headline "*Gilmore Girls*' Subtle Liberalism and Universal Empathy." I began to watch the *Girls* the same year Lehman Brothers collapsed, smack bang in the middle of the United States' war on the nebulous concept of "terror," so the argument would have credence, if not for the fact that 2008 was quite unlike much of the preceding decade.

I came to the show soon after the resounding electoral defeat of Australia's arch-conservative Prime Minister John Howard, the same year Barack Obama was elected with the hopeful call of "Yes We Can." Indeed, I would wake up at 3 a.m. mere weeks after bingeing *Gilmore Girls*' first three seasons to watch Obama's historic inauguration speech inside my cabin, a few clicks outside the coal mine. But Obama had never felt like my saviour, no United States president ever was. "Liberalism," in the colloquial Western sense, had, throughout my teens, placed itself in opposition to my faith practice. White liberals obsessed with saving me from my headscarf were almost more annoying than white conservatives who surveilled my every teenage move for a sign I was a terrorist in disguise.

At some level, I knew that if I had met Rory or Lorelai in person, they would not have folded me into their arms, welcoming me into the warm bosom of Luke's diner with a smile and a sly shout for "more coffee!" I was more likely to be a subject of their pity, a project to be worked on, a "teachable moment." Did you know there is a genocide happening in Darfur? I could imagine Rory asking me, after the revelation that I was born in Sudan, as if she were the first to bear this knowledge, the one to educate me about my own country. This rhetorical question would no doubt come hot on the heels of a comment Lorelai might make about "exotic African countries," or knowing about Sudan because she'd watched *The Last King of Scotland* and wasn't James McAvoy a total hunk and didn't I think it funny a film about a Ugandan dictator had Scotland in the title and do you think Ugandans drink coffee? They really should get onto that because who doesn't like coffee!

Given Uganda is one of the world's top producers of coffee, it is likely that Lorelai was drinking Ugandan beans in Luke's diner, but that only reinforces the point. I knew my real self would not have been a part of their world, in the same way I knew I was not actually part of the rural landscape of Dalby, nor the rough-and-tumble of the coal mine I had tried to claim as my own. I was securely an outsider in Queensland, as in Stars Hollow. Yet somehow, I still felt of it. How?

"*Gilmore Girls* . . . foregrounds a class-based conflict, articulated as a generational tension between the show's two primary families, the senior Gilmores, Emily and Richard . . . and the 'Gilmore girls,' their daughter, Lorelai . . . and granddaughter, Rory," writes Daniela Mastrocola in "Performing Class: *Gilmore Girls* and a Classless Neoliberal 'Middle Class.' " Mastrocola critiques Lorelai's "classless" depiction in the series, which she argues reinforces the "ambiguous neoliberal notion of a middle class."

Was there something about this plucky, not-quite-working-class dynamic that resonated with me? A family obsessed with doing things on their own terms, who believed education was the route to social mobility, a woman (in Lorelai) forced into contradiction out of a desire to provide for her daughter what she could not have for herself? I wondered if I saw something of my mother in both Emily and Lorelai, both the disciplinarian with sky-high expectations and the cheerleader with the belief that her daughter is capable of anything, everything, so long as she put her mind to it.

Alas, my attentions were not about the class dynamics, although Mastrocola's piece on the "classless neoliberal 'middle class' " has much to commend it. This was about what *Gilmore Girls* is always about. The impossibility, the contradiction, the incurability of being daughter. "Finitude is the daughter who will never catch up in time, in history, to the mother. The mother, the daughter—together these create a form of exchange, a form of the non-approach to the origin, the impossibility of catching up fully (and to that which we most adore)," says Eugenie Brinkema in "A Mother Is a Form of Time: *Gilm-ore Girls* and the Elasticity of In-Finitude" (2012). The show is, "in the end, a series about what it means to be a little too close, about the problem of boundaries and the impossibility some-times with family, with texts, and with television of knowing where one structure ends and the other starts."

Where did I begin and my mother end? At the tender age of seventeen, I wasn't sure, but I was downright afraid of know-ing the answer. I was a high-achieving young woman, but there was a part of me that feared any success I enjoyed was my mother's, any failure I suffered my own. I had founded a youth organisation, joined boards and been nominated for awards, but was that my own doing, or was I a mere cipher for my mother's ambitions? I had been commended for my activism and my voice, but was that my doing, or the result of oppor-tunities my mother had hustled for, magicked out of thin air, a visionary without the resources to build her dreams beyond the weak seedling she had birthed?

Where did my mother end and I begin? She was the "good" Sudanese woman, one who would have never taken the bus trip I did, never used a cuss word I enjoyed curling my tongue around, never have dreamed of ending up with a neck-tattooed coal miner, as I had done in the cool darkness of my cabin, time and time again. As I aged, I would learn of all my mother did that placed her outside the bands of "goodness" in the eyes of other Sudanese women. But for me, anything she did must be good, for she was mother.

What was "Mother" but "Good," and if Mother was Good,

what did that make me? Was daughter the extension of mother, or its opposite, its reflection, its contradiction? If Mother is Good, where do we allow for Mother to be human? Perhaps that is what made *Gilmore Girls* so compelling for me, all those years ago. Perhaps that is what remains potent, despite its politics, its whiteness, its unreality. The real shine of *Gilmore Girls* was less what it told me about myself, and more what it showed me of my mother. After all, while motherhood might be temporal, every mother is a daughter, and daughter is a permanent state.

I met my friend again recently, thousands of miles away from Dalby, with many Christmases now under my belt. We were older now, wiser, with our own questions about being mothers ourselves, although neither of us had yet to pass that threshold. Partway through the conversation, I mentioned I was writing this essay, my eyes full of nostalgia, hiding a shy request for permission I was not sure I needed.

Her sad laugh shocked me. "*Gilmore Girls* was my depression show," she said, her mouth twisting with the admission.

I choked on my water, unable to match her words with my recollection. "Really?" was all I could manage.

How could I not have seen it at the time? The hours we spent sharing her duvet, watching episode after episode of a fictional world where there are solutions to every challenge and the problem is never your brain chemistry or your metabolism. I thought of us watching the first season's Christmas episode while real-life Christmas swirled around us. The festive season had felt like a performance, but aren't we all always performing? Performing daughterhood, performing womanhood, performing goodness, performing self. While some might critique the performance as separate from reality, perhaps what *Gilmore Girls* taught me was performance, "surficiality," in the words of Eugenie Brinkema, is a "pure plane of being." Brinkema insists on the "value of the surface," claiming it "is not a plane to be broken, that richer treasures underneath might be mined, pillaged, and plundered, but that gloss, speed, sensation, and distance are themselves worthy of theoretical insight and time."

My friend's performance of wellness, my own performance of adventure, my mother's performance of contentment, the *Girls'* performance of it all. The surface, the performance, reality, worthy, in its own right. Therein lies the contradiction, and the beauty; the latter being the former, the former performing the latter, akin to a real-life Möbius strip.

Contradiction, and beauty. One a mother, one a daughter, the two both and neither, one and the same, wrapped up in infinitude.

Gilmore Girls—and Boys. It's a Mother-Son Thing

Freya North

Picture, if you will, the following scene.

It's late afternoon on a blustery day in early April 2023 and we are on a small farm in the English countryside. The farmhouse (simple but pretty, clad in wood, roof could do with a little repair, window frames need repainting) sits unassumingly in a meadow. There are buds on the orchard trees while puffs of early cherry blossom and hawthorn scent the hedgerow and birds sing the promise of spring. In the house, towering on a chair, is a pile of laundry that needs putting away, there's a garbage bag sitting inside the front door, mail lies unopened on the kitchen table, and next to it, a random shoe and an empty packet of potato chips. Yesterday's pots and pans have yet to be washed up. There isn't much in the fridge. Lore-lai Gilmore would feel right at home.

In the sitting room, the log burner is lit and two dogs sleep by the hearth. The TV is on and twenty-two-year-old Felix, home from university, is completely absorbed in a show on Netflix. Suddenly his mother, somewhat windswept and slightly wild about the eyes, makes a cyclonic entry into the house.

"Felix!"

No answer—he's captivated by drama unfolding on the screen.

"Felix!"

"Huh?" He turns his head a notch but his eyes remain fixed on the TV.

"I've been phoning and phoning you—you didn't pick up!"

She may as well be talking to thin air. She's kind of used to it. She talks at him at breakneck speed, recounting the chaos of her day, cramming a chocolate bar into her mouth while she picks up things and puts them down again and speaks with her mouth full and barely pauses for breath.

". . . Felix!!"

"Oh—soz—I was . . ." But he's held captive by a scene unfolding on the TV: a man is waiting outside a diner, inside there are numerous tins of paint, dust sheets all around, there's more than interior decorating on his mind. Whomever he's waiting on isn't going to show. Oh—hang on—that very person is currently entangled in a passionate embrace on a balcony elsewhere.

"Wait!" Felix's mother turns to face the screen. "But!

What?? *Gilmore Girls*?!" She regards her son with amazement. "You're watching *Gilmore Girls*? You?"

"I'm obsessed," Felix shrugs happily in the vague direction of his mother. "It's us," he tells her. "Actually, it's more than just us. It's who I was when I was younger—who I am now—who I'll become one day."

In an instant, his mother forgets about her stressy day and all the idiots in it, the various items on the to-do list she was phoning her son about and the various items strewn around the house that need sorting and all about her stroppy mood in general. Instead, she sits herself down beside him and they watch three more episodes back-to-back, only breaking for dinner when they're overcome with emotion because Emily Gilmore is overcome with emotion visiting the tiny hut Lorelai and Rory first lived in.

True story, that.

Here's what I find interesting about the enduring and cross-generational appeal of *Gilmore Girls*. My son Felix was in his final year at university, taking a joint-honours degree in English + Film Studies, when he discovered the show. He was in the midst of researching and writing his thesis, entitled "Essential Critique or Dangerous Endorsement: The Satirical Representation of Toxic Masculinity in *Fight Club* and *American Psycho*." Previously, he and I had watched all six seasons of *The Sopranos* as part of his course. He goes to watch each John Wick movie at the cinema on the day of release.

Ultimately, though, it isn't Christian Bale or Brad Pitt he'd choose to hang out with, nor does he want to check into the

Continental Hotel. He doesn't crave a capicola sandwich with Tony and Paulie and Silvio at Satriale's Pork Store in New Jersey. For a twenty-two-year-old lad, Stars Hollow had become his definitive happy place, its inhabitants his support network, while he tackled the stress and workload of university. What Felix wanted was to be in Connecticut, sitting at the counter at Luke's having a banter and burger. I'm not sure that Amy Sherman-Palladino wrote the show with the Felix Type in mind—but *Gilmore Girls* continues to resonate with him on many levels, providing more than entertainment, bringing him solace and respite and light relief and companionship.

I had come across the show independently from my son on one of those evenings when I'd been aimlessly zapping through the myriad offerings competing across the streaming services. I vaguely remembered the title from many years before and I decided to dip in and give it my "twenty-minute rule." Over 110 hours later, it appears I'm in it for the long haul. But on that day last April, with an uncanny dynamic befitting Lorelai and Rory, it transpired that Felix and I were just one episode apart in season 1.

The two of us remain completely united in our commitment to the show. It's a mother-son thing. *Gilmore Girls* belongs to us. Anytime he was home for a weekend break or the vacations from university, he and I would teleport to Stars Hollow and reconvene with our friends, who were delighted to see us again. So much had happened since we last saw them, and yet, comfortingly, nothing much had changed.

Full disclosure: at the time of writing, Felix and I have yet to finish the show (a luxury awaiting us which will place us at the envy of many readers of this book). We have an unspoken rule to only ever watch *Gilmore Girls* together, which has necessitated extreme self-restraint not to sneak in extra episodes if one of us isn't around. Sometimes, we've had to endure weeks of *Gilmore* famine. Currently, we're gorging season 6 with eighteen episodes to go. However, when it comes to this essay, I warned the editor that I would *not* be rushing through the seasons to have it all watched. I would *not* be IMDBing or googling or Redditing *a single thing* about the show. You know how Lorelai drives her car? That's me in my determination to steer clear and speed away from all spoilers. I'd rather have Lane wallop her drums two feet away from me than unwittingly hear even a snippet of What. Happens. Next. The only thing I have searched online (obsessively, I'll admit) is: LORELAI GILMORE CLOTHES OUTFITS TOPS BOOTS WHERE TO BUY SHOPPING SHIP TO UK.

What is it about this show which has found its way under my skin and woven through not just my heart but my son's too? What are our shared points of reference—and what confronts us separately on differing but profound levels? Yes of course Felix and I sit together and laugh and wince and cheer and gasp because the writing is so good, the humour so razor sharp it could split logs, a setting so enviable we want to relocate, characters so known to us we can't quite believe we're not in a WhatsApp group with the lot of them. Yes, we marvel at the retro coolness of all those vintage gadgets that were cutting edge at the time—from pagers to flip phones to the colourful clamshell iBooks. Obviously, I point out *how young* Jack from *This Is Us* looks, while Felix enlightens me as to what Dean and Kirk went on to do next under their different names. Predictably, we play spot-the-guest-star-before-they-were-famous, and it goes without saying how we love that Sookie became Melissa McCarthy. But reader, it goes way deeper than such surface details.

I'm a single mother and it's been that way since Felix and his younger sister Georgia were tiny. So, on a very personal level, this show is my show. When I started watching *Gilmore Girls*, I'd already gone through the teenage years with my off-spring and come out the other side—so I'd call across to the TV, offering Lorelai my advice and support because I'd been there, done that and somehow survived. Now, in just nine months and five seasons of sublimely entertaining time-travel, Rory is currently twenty-one and so is my daughter—which means that Lorelai and I must have experienced everything in tandem and I don't think I've ever felt so close to a fictitious character. I am as grateful to the writers for drawing from life and detailing the flaws and the loneliness, the freedom and the fear and the joy of lone parenting, as I am to Lauren Graham for portraying so convincingly the stumbling passage that us single mums make in our (frequently misdirected) bid to ensure that our kids are okay. With just a fleeting facial tick, one tear-stung eye, a teeth-clench of exasperation, a lip sucked hard to bite down on emotion or to silence a hasty rebuke, Lorelai shows how I feel. I hear me in her tone of voice. Throughout the five-and-a-bit seasons I've watched, I've seen how Lorelai, too, fears that the world will take her child away from her, the potentially dangerous and way-too-big world, whilst also finding the courage to let that child leave.

But, at its core, this is a show where no one is all bad and no one is all good. Stars Hollow, as quaint as it is, is also restrictive and bland, and some people come and they don't stay, whilst others find that they can't leave. And—oh Emily. Emily provides Felix and me with toe-curling and face-twisting moments when we squirm and need to watch through our fingers due to the glare of her unbridled awfulness and snobbery.

Midway through season 5, we had to admit defeat with the challenge we'd set to keep count of how many maids Emily's been through—yet both of us felt so acutely her sense of abandonment and shame when Rory turns from her while Lorelai is already estranged. In Emily's company, Lorelai frequently behaves like a recalcitrant and moody teenager, but actually, I do that to my own mum (who's nothing like Emily, I hasten to add). It's not a good look on Lorelai, and it made me realize it's not a good look on me either. And, actually, sometimes Lorelai deserves the sharp edge of Emily's tongue; she's in the wrong— and her mother is the one to put her right because that's what mothers need to do.

Mums and daughters, mums and daughters. I have gently envied Lorelai and Rory their chumminess, the way they can converse at such length, their closeness and trust and their confidence that even if they show each other their ugly sides, love isn't compromise. There have been times when I've wanted to say to my own daughter, Oh for heaven's sake why

can't you Be More Rory. I'm sure my daughter wishes I'd cut
her the slack Lorelai offers Rory, and that our kitchen had the
junk food/vegetable ratio of theirs.

Gilmore Girls holds a mirror to life whilst also providing a
breather from reality, and therein lies its enduring quality.
There is realism and super-realism, mundanity and cartoon-
ery, pathos and sadness, laughter and tears. As well as hitting the mark so perfectly by oversizing the portrayal of true
feelings and the understandable reactions real people would
have, *Gilmore Girls* delivers essential escapism. It's a show
about day-to-day life and yet it is only a show, and, by defi-
nition, an escape from day-to-day life. It gives me everything
I need. Every single trope is defiantly there—as the very first
episode unfolds, we know that everything will work out for
every single character: sorry times will befall them along the
way, unwise choices will be made and the wrong paths taken,
but in the end, good will triumph over bad and there will be
happy-ever-after. In Stars Hollow, ultimately, the right thing
will happen. It's not the real world—but true dilemmas and
sincere emotions live there.

Of course, no one should allow their young kid to drink
so much coffee, or raise them on candy alone. But, famously,
it takes a village to raise a child, and Stars Hollow has done
admirably by Rory. Just as Lorelai has superbright Rory, so,
too, am I similarly blessed with Felix. I know from the fre-
quent sideways glances he'll send over whilst we're watching
the show that he sees me in Lorelai—whether it's a beseeching
gaze for me to Be More Lorelai or a raised eyebrow that says

See What I Have to Go Through. So I asked him to jot me a few notes about why he loves *Gilmore Girls* and why the show works for a young man in his early twenties when it aired the year before he was born and finished when he was just six years old. I was hoping he'd proselytise about its importance in providing such quality time for him and his old mum to share. He didn't. But this is what he said.

> An integral part of *Gilmore Girls'* success comes from its innate sense of familiarity without sacrificing comedy. The characters and situations are all necessarily exaggerated for comedic effect, and yet the show never seems outlandish to a level of disconnect. Characters such as Kirk or Miss Patty may on paper seem absurd, yet to most (especially those who have lived in a small town akin to Stars Hollow) they are immediately recognisable.
>
> Where a lesser show would be content with leaving the supporting cast as one-note jokes, *Gilmore Girls* combines the absurdity with nuance and genuine heart, making even the most dislikeable of characters (ahem, Taylor, ahem) thoroughly lovable. *Gilmore Girls* truly embodies the philosophy of laughing with, not "at", the characters; the stories may be somewhat far-fetched or predictable, the characters outlandish, but the familiarity that courses through the blood of the show makes it all seem real.
>
> It's not a show one simply watches, rather you become part of the cast, you live the events alongside the char-

acters and truly get to know them. By the time you finish the show, you find yourself far from an observer
of the Gilmore girls' antics; you've become one of
them yourself.

Had Rory reviewed the show for the *Yale Daily News*, I rather
think that's pretty much what she'd have written. Lorelai—you
and I need to get our kids together.

Guilty Gilmores of a Parallel Universe

Anjanette Delgado

From the start, everything about *Gilmore Girls* annoyed me: The alliterative title. The too-perky mom with whose youthful exuberance I couldn't compete. Her impossibly well-behaved daughter. The Christmas-postcard town where no one went hungry and nothing truly terrible ever happened. Plus, who talked that fast without help from drugs? But they begged, my daughters, excited to have found a TV show we could watch together after months of me working longer hours than usual, justifying my neglect with fatigue and unpaid bills. They were thirteen and ten at the time and I felt on the cusp of losing them, the girls they'd been, maybe still were: trusting, loving, ever-forgiving.

So I gave in and watched despite story lines that insisted on reminding me of all the mothering I'd done with nothing approaching grace; that dredged the cluttered backyard of my harried mind, my wheel spoke of memories so long covered up I was shocked when the fictional world of Stars Hollow pulled up real-life feelings. Uncomfortable feelings. Guilty, guilty feelings.

From "The Reigning Lorelai" (season 4, episode 16):
RICHARD GILMORE: You only have one set of parents, Lorelai. Remember that.

CAROLINA, PUERTO RICO • 1974

The tiny room is so dark, I can't see her, even though our twin beds face each other, only inches apart. I am seven; my sister's four, and so skinny that when she sleeps, she more sighs in morose beats than snores, her scrawny chest rising and falling in gentle sync with her breath. I know this, but I make no attempt to confirm, focused instead on listening for what woke me. The dull thud I pray I've dreamt this time, then hear again, duller now, like a book dropped hard on the floor.

There's a yelp like a dog's, my memory of it still pristine. The sound meant he was home, back from a job he found demeaning, playing the sax for tourists in San Juan. Through the wall, I distinguish his voice. I can't understand the words, but they're clipped at the end like blows, and I know it's trouble, my chest rising and falling like my sister's, but faster. Then I hear my mother, the begging inflection, her words scratchy, the yelper identified.

Eyes now accustomed to darkness, I make out my sister's body, still asleep despite the noise from the next room. I go to the edge of her bed and lie down, wanting to be an extra buffer. For her. Then I press open palms over my ears with all my might, and eventually fall back to sleep to the muffled rhythm of my father's bloody music.

Weeks later, we escaped to New York. As the plane lifts, I glance at my mother, sandwiched between us. I tell her she's so pretty, promise I'll be good, get good grades. She smiles and puts a finger to her lips so I know takeoff is important and we must be quiet. It's my first flight, but I'm not afraid; I'm relieved. She's taken us along, rescued us, and I'm so grateful just then, I could climb right back into her womb from love.

From "That Damn Donna Reed" (season 1, episode 14):
(Cut to Lorelai getting home. She looks in the chicken
    cage—it's empty.)
LORELAI: [. . .] OK, that's OK. I can fix this. We can fix this.
(LORELAI GOES TO THE PHONE.)
LORELAI: I'm going to make this better. I'm going to fix—
HELLO?
LUKE: Yeah.
LORELAI: Luke?

Thirty years later, it's 2004 and I'm living in a universe of broken things that cannot be fixed, my girls and me trapped in the town of Too Late because I disciplined or forbade when I should've understood, or I criticized too quickly, or failed to realize the sweet girl I pushed them to befriend was a bully who'd leave long-lasting scars. Because I was (take your pick) exasperated, tired, absent, asleep, or there-but-not-really-listening as Leah and Vee starved for attention right in front of me.

It's why I keep watching long after the girls dramatically pronounce themselves "over" *Gilmore Girls* sometime after season 3. Because unlike in my world, things got fixed, were forgiven, or talked through, in Stars Hollow. Granted they weren't generally the worst things, but even when they were—teen pregnancy, bullying, functional alcoholism—affection for others and common decency made them okay in the end, sappy as that sounds. And coffee. Nothing was ever hopeless or ruined if there was coffee.

I came to need that, the show's fix of quirky charm and unassailable love, even though it came with a hefty dose of guilt. The more I watched Lorelai make adorably fixable mistakes, her heart always in precisely the right place, the more firmly tethered I became to my parallel of regret, wondering how I'd managed to mess up so badly as a mother, when all I ever wanted was to be a better mom than my own had been.

CAROLINA, PUERTO RICO • 1981

I used to love my mother. Not as I do now. Because of duty, a shared history. To not be a woman who doesn't cherish her own mother. No, I loved her. Her smell, how she posed for photos, getting in place, and flashing her bright white gap-toothed smile the second anyone said "cheese," "whiskey," or "panties."

I admired her, too, for raising herself from the age of ten when her own mother developed a form of highly functional schizophrenia. For how tender she was with her, teaching us to love Monse even though she rarely recognized us and, toward the end, would accuse us of stealing her long-gone husband, calling us "dirty little whores" when we were barely out of elementary school.

And now, what I don't want to say, but must if I want you to understand my mother's crime. But I'll be quick, as if you and I were Lorelai and Rory, launching into one of the rapid back-and-forths of witty inaneness with which we've composed the song of our unique "friends first, mother-daughter second" bond.

Okay. We're at Luke's, the sun filtering through the slightly grimy picture-glass window, tall mugs of steaming coffee before us:

From Parallel-Universe Gilmore Girls' "Divorce Bounty" (season 0, episode 0):

YOU (AS RORY): Spill.

ME (AS LORELAI): Nothing to spill. Three years later, we went back.

YOU: Oh no. Why?

ME: An elderly aunt of my mom's couldn't keep taking care of Monse.

YOU: Were you scared?

ME: Terrified. But my mom said she had to face him, divorce him.

YOU: And did she?

ME: She did, and then my sister and I were court-ordered to live with him on weekends.

YOU: Oh no!

ME: Worse.

YOU (KNOWING): Payback.

ME (SHRUGGING): Yep. He'd terrify us, scream, make threats against our mom. When my sister had enough, she refused to return, but I was too afraid, too much of a people-pleaser, so . . .

YOU: So?

ME: Other things. Bad things.

YOU: Oh. And . . . you didn't tell?

ME: I was ashamed. Thought I'd done the bad things with him. Sometimes, I still feel I, somehow, allowed them.

YOU: So sorry.

ME: Yeah. Me too.

Less than a year after divorcing, they were back together.

Weeks after that, he was at it again.

Christmas Eve, I was screeching for anyone passing by the house to help my mother. But my father kicked me down before anyone stopped, then continued kicking my face, breaking my lips open in so many places my mouth was a stomped-on rosebud for days. The worst part was having to sit on our beds all through that night, our twin beds facing each other, inches away, and listen to him thud, kick, punch, and smack in the next room. Every twenty or thirty minutes, he'd let it die down, then start again, an extra layer of cruelty our neighbors must have heard but did nothing about. By dawn, we were asleep, his blood music silent, darkness giving way to Christmas morning.

On the January day school reopened after the holiday recess, I waited for the bell to ring, for everyone to head to homeroom, then went into the school counselor's office and told her everything. What my father did to my mother, to us. What he did to me when he sent my mom and my sister out on errands.

The school counselor listened, her eyes opening so wide as I talked as to seem impossibly big behind her cat-eye tortoise-shell frames. Then, she excused herself to talk to someone. When she returned, she told me we could be removed into a home for orphans or into foster care. Did I want that? I thought of my little sister who barely snored and made me laugh and told her I did.

Under threat from the school, my mother kicked my father out even though he denied everything that had to do with me. Now he couldn't be in the house with us because if I was hurt, or disappeared, the school would send the police. I thought we were saved.

Until my mother began to ask questions. The same ones, again and again, as if to catch me in a lie. I was thirteen by then. Did I just want more freedom to do teenage things? Is that why I'd said those awful things? I maintained I had told the truth but wouldn't give her more details or repeat the ones I'd told the school counselor. Her questions were like knife wounds. The images in my head, close-range shame gunshots.

But she kept asking, growing angrier, sometimes screaming at me to get out of her house, reminding me of Monse demanding I show shame for being the filthy child whore who'd stolen her husband.

After I told, she drank daily and cried for no discernible reason. She gained weight and quit her job and listened to loud music in the mornings and cleaned the house late at night and wanted to love me but couldn't help hating me. I decided if my mother was going to hate me for what wasn't my fault, then I'd hate her right back, act as I pleased, move out the moment I reached legal age.

To make my getaway, I juggled several after-school jobs, including an overnight shift inserting flyers at a local paper, after which I took a bus to school, drinking Gilmore-girl amounts of coffee to stay awake throughout my day.

One morning, I skipped school and headed home from my overnight shift at the paper, hoping to sleep. I'd already been chosen class valedictorian and reasoned that missing a day would be okay. But it wasn't, because I saw it even before the bus let me off a few feet away from our tiny concrete square of a house: my father's maroon Mustang, drizzled in dew. Reeling, I walked to the corner pay phone. She picked up immediately, repeating a suspicious "Hello?" several times before I hung up.

Her house still sits in front of a ballpark, and that morning, I walked to an empty dugout to watch what until then I'd considered my home—his car parked in front of it, as if to claim it, and decided I would single-handedly rewrite our family's history of women driven crazy by men: I'd get my own place, have my own daughters, and raise them better than she'd raised us.

From "Let Me Hear Your Balalaikas Ringing Out" (season 6, episode 8):

LORELAI: I did this all wrong. [...] Why can't I fix these things?

LUKE: Hey.

LORELAI: I'm a bad mother!

LUKE: You're not a bad mother.

MIAMI, FLORIDA · 2000

I didn't raise my daughters better. I ruined it from the start. Barely eighteen, I looked for a Ken to place in my pink camper, a placeholder to label "the dad": handsome, decent job, slightly older, but given to humor and play. A man who wasn't violent, who'd be unable to control me, whose brain I could circle in formation, the better to keep our future daughters safe.

Pregnant at nineteen, I thought, No problem. I'll work full time, go to night college, take care of my baby. Two years later, pregnant with Leah, I celebrated the end of my relationship. I'd been unwilling to let him have a say in anything related to the raising of Vee, unwilling to allow any disciplining of my rambunctious two-year-old, loath to let him decide anything in "our lives," which to me included only Vee and me, and now Leah. Rather than see it as the mistake it had been, I was excited to have them to myself. I'd just work harder, give them everything whether he helped or not. I'd be a great single mother. Much better than . . . well, I'd show her.

Instead, by the end of its run, I'm mostly watching *Gilmore Girls* to see Lorelai mess up worse than I have. But she doesn't. Instead, she knows to live in a small town where her kid is safer, and the community supports her. She destroys my top excuse: that being a single mother who works, I am exhausted and don't have the energy to listen. Lorelai is always dog-tired and listens. She's present. She showers her daughter with attention and isn't flattened when she remembers being wrong about everything, most of all about how it would be "easy" to be a good mother because she was going to "work really hard" to be one. That's how I set myself up for the impossible task of being Lorelai Gilmore. I made myself "it." I chose, cavalierly, stupidly, to be all my daughters had before I was old enough to know who I was, who I might be.

Before I had dreams or any idea of the space those dreams might fight my children to occupy. Of course, it wasn't like that at first. No, at first, I was on it. Every day. Every year. I married my lovely girls and loved being everything at all times. I danced with them, made art and played dress-up and Monopoly, helped with homework, drove to activities and sleepovers, made pancakes for dinner, and was always excited to go for large library book hauls. Which is to say I did love them and worked hard to protect them from others. I just didn't protect them enough from me.

And then, in their teens, just when they needed me the

most, I ran out of gas and it was as if there were two women inside me: one who felt trapped and wanted to fly away, to exist on a silent cloud where she could just be free, maybe even start over, while the other cried nonstop for the children she was running away from.

This is my crime. I had children to prove my mother wrong for not choosing me. To be right. But motherhood is the longest sainthood, and when I did this, I stole from my girls. They were (are) beautiful, funny, loud-snoring, smart, witty, kindhearted, feisty, wide-eyed, innocent girls, and they needed more than my physical body and the restlessness of my reluctant gaze. They deserved more than that obnoxious know-it-all. That angry, loudmouthed, easily stressed girl who was so scared all the time. Scared of losing control of them, and scared of the world of men that made keeping them safe all the harder.

Underneath everything, of course, was what I never said out loud but thought: that at least I wasn't my mother, choosing a bad man over my own daughters. That, I see now, was a weak excuse, not even good enough for a parallel universe. My Lorelai was as guilty of choosing an "other" (writing, resting, escaping) over her children as my mother's Emily had been.

MIAMI, FLORIDA   ·   1991–2016

It happens slowly. For years, I act as if I don't really have a mother. As if there's a lady who is my daughters' grandmother, and she loves them, but I don't fully trust her with them any more than she trusted Monse with me.

Still, I have a duty as a daughter, so I do it: perfunctory
fifteen-minute calls every two weeks; a monthly contribution
to the ever-increasing bills of a woman growing old alone; and
Christmas, birthday, and Mother's Day gifts, always accom-
panied by a card expressing the appropriate sentiment for the
occasion, so she can't accuse me of being mean. Her drinking doesn't help. My inability to forgive her helps less. When
she offers advice, I reject it. When she sends a gift, a sacrifice
on her fixed income, I tell her thanks, she shouldn't have, and
make sure to withhold any joy I might feel over whatever she
was so excited to give me.

Sometime in the early 2010s, she breaks down. I am in
Puerto Rico for work and have taken the afternoon off to visit
her before taking a plane back to Miami.

"Yo te he hecho mucho daño," she says.

I have harmed you so much.

When she says it, she's crying. She's also been drinking.
Still, I'm astonished to hear the words, though I brush them
aside under the guise of needing to make my flight. But they
move me. Dislodge something inside me so that I now feel my
hard places, can touch the ridges on the surface of the boulder I've turned myself into over the years. With everyone. Men
I dated, friends, coworkers, the world at large. My daughters.

One day in 2015, I ask my mother to stop drinking. "It's just
a starting point," I say. But she does it, building sober months
out of sober days. To encourage her, I start to call weekly to talk
about unimportant things.

We get better. Not perfect, but at least now we flow on the

phone, even though we know our refound connection depends on neither one of us ever talking to the other about what still hurts.

Meanwhile, the girls are now fifteen and seventeen, and I am intent on retightening my bond with them. I begin letting "surefire" ideas for the next great Puerto Rican novel go unwritten if it means interrupting or tuning out my daughters. I figure out how to be soft, how not to protect myself from them, even though I know no one can hurt me like they can. I even make an effort to assume it's all working, ignoring their inscrutable "whatever" and "as-if" teenage faces.

Some days are, of course, easier than others. I tell my best friend, Migdalia, about *Gilmore Girls*, and about Lorelai, the "perfect" mother. Migdalia seems puzzled for a beat, then says: "Well, of course she's perfect. She's a fictional character. You and I have to live in the real world."

From "There's the Rub" (season 2, episode 16):
EMILY: [. . .] And because of this we have no relationship.
LORELAI: Oh, Mom, we have a relationship.
EMILY: We do? What? What is our relationship?
LORELAI: W-well, w-we . . .
EMILY: *Exactly.*

MIAMI, FLORIDA · NOVEMBER 25, 2016
My mother is visiting us in Miami for the first time in eight years. We've done the dishes after a lunch of Puerto Rican Thanksgiving leftovers—pork, arroz con gandules, pump-

kin flan—and I'm looking forward to the final-final season of
Gilmore Girls: A Year in the Life, which premiered overnight. But
Leah's asleep on the couch, and Vee, headphones on, begs off,
pointing at my mother and making silent yakking motions
followed by praying ones that ask me to save her from her
grandma's relentless questions.

I am elated. Vee's conspiratorial gesture is a sign, the first
since I began to work on us. Or maybe elated is not the right
word. Maybe it's happiness: lack of regret mixed with hope.
"What's that?" my mother asks as I pull up Netflix on the house
desktop, changing audio language to Spanish, setting up cap-
tions for English.

"A show."

"I know it's a show. You gonna watch it with that face?"

"What face?"

"That one! Like punishment."

I touch my face, feel what she means. Even though I invited
her, it's been hard to breathe since she arrived, and my face
shows the toll of battle between resentment and forgiveness. I
have built up to this visit—reading, meditating, looking at old
photos, and even making lists of all the things for which I'm
grateful to her—but now, having her here, in my space, threatens to remind me that I couldn't be happy in hers, places all
those old useless feelings on my face for her to see.

"It's *Gilmore Girls*. We watched when the girls were little,
kind of taught us how to fit in,

here, in Florida," I spin.

She searches my eyes. I don't know what she wants from me.

"Wanna watch?" I ask.

"You don't want me here," she says after a few seconds.

And I see that she, too, is struggling. Suffering. I don't want her to suffer. It's not that I don't want to be the daughter who brings her mother to her house only to make her sad. It's that it pains me to hurt her because I love her. It's a weathered love. A scared love. But, in that moment, it is love.

I pat the seat next to me.

"It's in English," she protests, but her face relaxes.

"Ah, but behold the magic of streaming audio translation," I say.

"The what?" she asks, grimacing, but gathers her printed housedress, the large gap between her front teeth barely showing, and her hand stretching as if to reach for my forearm, hovering over it for a second before she pulls it back, sitting next to me and reclining instead, her green summer flip-flops falling off her feet.

MIAMI, FLORIDA, AND CAROLINA, PUERTO
RICO   •   NOVEMBER 2016 AND JULY 2023

The next time I am in Puerto Rico, I don't tell her. Not at first. I catch up with old friends, wander the streets of Old San Juan, and fall asleep at La Esquina, a bookstore within a seventies-era apartment in the college neighborhood of Santa Rita, with a terrace full of potted plants and a floor fan pointed at the mid-century settee where it lulls me with equal parts breeze and heat. I want to have Puerto Rico to myself, to let it have me to itself before I call my mother, start seeing everything through her eyes. And the thing is, I have reasons. That last visit didn't end with my mother's flip-flops on the floor. It ended with Leah interviewing her about the family's history of major illnesses, my idea. It ended when she mentioned heart disease and let it slip that every morning, Leah's grandfather has to take a huge pill that he keeps in his medicine chest.

Leah doesn't seem to notice the change in the air. When she goes to her room, I turn to my mother.

"How do you know?" I ask.

"How do I know what?" she replies, though I can see she knows she has stepped in it, flip-flops and all.

"How do you know what my father has in his medicine cabinet?"

She says, "I don't." Says she hasn't seen him in over a year, that she never wants to see

him again.

I want to say a lot of things, but I just say, "Well, at least now I know for sure you've

never believed me. Do you understand I'm in my fifties? That I have no reason to lie?"

She doesn't answer.

I wait for her to explain, to say something that fixes things and makes me want to jump back into her womb from love. I want her to ask me how I am, why I still feel the need to talk about this. But she doesn't. Instead she begs me to leave things be, to not rouse old dust, to let things die.

I'm wondering if they are, now, in fact, dead, and that's when she says them, the words I work to forgive every day: He's an old man. In his eighties. In bad health. While I'm happy now, aren't I? My life is good? Shouldn't I just forgive and forget, then? Shouldn't I make an effort, muster the mercy to let my father die in peace?

But this isn't Stars Hollow. It isn't even a heartwarming TV series. This is us: me and my mother, frozen in time in my sweltering kitchen in Miami, unable to heal, so many years of pain and betrayal between us, even Lorelai Gilmore couldn't fix us if she tried.

Could Watching *Gilmore Girls* Make Me Normal?

My Quest to Find Out

Cathi Hanauer

I grew up not in a *No TV* household so much as a *Selective TV* household, with the selection revolving around the tastes and whims of my Type A father. We could watch television only with permission, and we weren't allowed daytime TV except for *Batman*—because it was on from 5:30 to 6:00, when my mother was whipping up the beef Stroganoff or turkey à la king for our family of six.

On Sunday nights, homework or not, we were ordered to the den for *Masterpiece Theatre*—to make us "cultured"—and we all watched *The French Chef*, so that my mother, and perhaps we daughters, too, could learn to make boeuf bourguignon and chocolate mousse for our current or future husbands. I also was permitted to join my father for televised sporting events. So while I can still recite the names of the entire Oakland A's World Series-winning baseball team in 1973—and know how to fold egg whites into soufflé batter—I had, and still have, no idea about *Maude* or *M*A*S*H*, *Gilligan's Island* or *The Addams Family*. (This made me a freak at school; I survived childhood largely because my best friend's house, where I escaped whenever possible, featured a nonstop loop of *I Love Lucy* and the shopping channel.)

What *was* valued over "junky" TV in my house—encouraged or required by my father, along with school—was reading, especially books. Not *all* books, mind you, but the "good" ones that "smart" people read: Dickens, Steinbeck, Updike, Philip Roth, even John Irving. (As with TV, a mainstream selection could be tossed in occasionally and still make the "Approved" list.) Newspapers also were eventually mandatory; less the local paper, with its comic strips and dog look-alike contests, than the *New York Times* and its coverage of politics, business, war. Never mind that I was young, female (little from these books or news was weighted toward girls), and, though I did well in school, more a "popular" than studious type—e.g., more interested in being a twirler (because the skirt? with those cute ankle boots??) than joining the debate team or science club, yawn. The point is, with all this reading, there was even less time for watching TV, except for, say it with me, *The French Chef* and *Masterpiece Theatre* (and *Batman*).

Perhaps unpredictably, my psycho childhood led me not to a rebellious adult life of endlessly bingeing from today's nine million streaming channels, but instead to a quiet view of television as somehow lowbrow and unworthy, at least compared to books—except in rare cases of venerated excellence (*Mad Men*, *The Sopranos*) or bizarre anomaly (*The Golden Bachelor*—loved!). My youth also probably helped turn me into a *writer* of those books—someone who now lives alone, toils independently, wears the same "comfortable clothes" (read: sleepwear) every day, and basically functions slightly outside of conventional society.

So when I was invited to write an essay about the popular show *Gilmore Girls*, I was delighted. With the guilt-zapping excuse of paid work, I could dive into mainstream American TV, emerging perhaps a little more "normal"—even with the twenty-six books (plus Kindle) currently dwarfing my nightstand. After all, the average American, according to a quick Google search, watches between three and four-*plus* hours of TV a day (a stat that, not gonna lie, stunned me). Plus, living in a New York City apartment with a view of cars exiting the Cross Bronx Expressway, I welcomed the foray into small-town charm. And I'd finally get to sample that show about the three old women that everyone was always referencing.

Turns out the three-old-women show was *The Golden Girls*, not *Gilmore Girls*, but no biggie; once I found the latter on Netflix and got my ex to hook me up as an "extra member" on his account, I sat down eagerly to watch. Skepticism on hold, SkinnyPop in hand, dog on couch next to me (wondering what was happening, as I never sat on the couch—only at my computer or in bed reading), I approached the show fresh, no research. I didn't want spoilers. I wanted to watch it as an actual viewer might have when it came out back in 2000.

Right away, I warmed to the pilot: sexy guy (Luke), intelligent woman (Lorelai) with her mature and compelling daughter (Rory), lively diner with copious coffee, Carole King theme song about best friends. The show featured mostly white, straight, and cisgendered characters and actors—Michel, the hilarious French concierge, is both brown-skinned and (clearly) gay, and teenage Lane is not just Korean but comprises an entire (very funny) subplot because of this—but otherwise, so much for diversity. But hey. This was small-town Connecticut more than two decades ago, complete with hayrides, snowman contests, and mandatory all-community meetings. Plus, the writers later spoof the place with that pack of Range Rover-driving moms who all have the exact same short blond bob (hilarious!), so okay. I moved on.

The show's main theme also enticed me: mother and daughter best friends, not far apart in age, with the serious, studious daughter often more sensible than her slightly boho, once-teen-mom single mother. I have a daughter myself with whom I've always been close, and it would be fun to see how we compared to Lorelai and Rory, who live in adorable Stars Hollow and hang out together, feasting on Pop-Tarts, takeout, and pancakes at the diner. There are regular love interests for both—about which they openly share details with each other—leading to steamy sexual tension. There are also, of course, quirky neighbors and store owners, town troubadours, and a kooky but talented chef (played by Melissa McCarthy, who steals the show in every scene she's in).

It's a vast cast of lovable oddballs, with mother and daughter teammates and confidantes among them, and I found the antics, no matter how minor, somehow always riveting.

Watching TV is so much fun! I thought on the third or maybe sixth night, as I clicked past the theme song for my fourth episode in a row, bleary-eyed and bloated with popcorn. I still wasn't sure this qualified as "worthy TV"—it definitely wasn't *Masterpiece Theatre*—but it was so wonderfully *female*, with the manic banter, endless food talk, constant love mishegoss. So what if the dialogue often seemed more "written" than realistic, more *fast* than actually meaningful or important?

The mother-daughter stuff didn't feel convincing to me: no sixteen-year-old girl, I thought—even in a wholesome small town—would put up with the teasing and invading Rory regularly takes from Lorelai, or the hypermanagement by her grandparents. (At least, *my* daughter wouldn't.) And the characters all sounded similar, if a few more shrill (the droll Paris) and a few less loquacious (all the men, except Michel). The minor players often felt like stereotypes or caricatures: uptight Kirk, the job-hopping nerd; lusty has-been-but-happy dance teacher Miss Patty; Babette, Lorelai's cat-loving neighbor who talks like she hails from a cross between Queens and deep New Jersey. (Later, I was tickled to read that these two talented women first acted together in *All in the Family*; even *I* recall a young Sally Struthers as ditzy Gloria.) Still: minor criticisms, no doubt typical of mainstream TV. I cheerfully accepted them.

I did, however, wonder how long I'd be at this; the episodes clocked in at around forty-five minutes each, and after days of watching, I was still on season 1. So I did some quick research... and almost had a heart attack. *Seven* seasons? At—wait—*twenty-two* episodes per season?? Not even including the 2016 four-part revival, *Gilmore Girls: A Year in the Life*. Had I really signed up for 150 or so hours of this?

Reader, I had.

My childhood conditioning kicked in. Even for a work assignment—and even in my quest to be a "normal gal" type who settles down for some chill TV after a long day—was this really a decent investment of my time? What would my father think of my spending prime *reading* hours each night watching Luke and Lorelai dance around the should-we-shouldn't-we question, surrounded by diner doughnuts and French fries? And did that matter? I was a grown woman, after all—and yet, childhood conditioning runs deep, even with the years of requisite therapy for someone like me.

So I decided to conduct a poll of my Sophisticated Friends and Relatives—the type I figured might not even watch TV, let alone this sort of program—to see if they knew of the show, and if so, to get their opinion. "Oh, I *adore Gilmore Girls*!" said my NPR reporter colleague, who broadcasts on such topics as foster care abuse and war-related PTSD. "My daughter and I watched *all the time* as she grew up. No matter what else was happening, when we climbed in bed together and turned it on, we felt comforted and bonded." "My patients *love* that show," said my psychoanalyst friend in Manhattan. "They find it soothing. Small-town America and all that." A third friend—critically acclaimed novelist—pronounced it "like crack." A fourth told me her entire family watched, due to its cross-generational appeal. "Something for everyone," she said. "Even grandparents."

After that, I gave over; my books could wait, and who cared if the show was lowbrow, highbrow, or no brow at all? Splayed on my couch, muscles atrophying, empty popcorn bags littering the floor, I would embrace this American TV classic that everyone and their mother, literally, seemed to adore. After all, the female main characters were all such eye candy, with their Gatorade-blue orbs. The coffee obsession was silly (but as a writer myself, I understood that it upped the Cozy factor), and the fixation on Harvard and Yale nauseating . . . but maybe the clearly kick-ass creator, Amy Sherman-Palladino, was going somewhere with it? And I found Lorelai compelling—her brainy goofiness combined with her raven-haired-Barbie-with-a-pout vibe, her cool clothes that hugged her tall, shapely body, her foray into teal and emerald eye shadow. I now looked forward to my eight-plus hours of TV a day, interrupted only by field trips to Target—to shop for eye shadow, obviously. I considered going darker at my next hair color.

That's when I realized I wanted to *be* Lorelai—well dressed, social, intelligent verging on intellectual (read: book-smart but without ever seeming to read), business-savvy yet gener-ous with her time for her beloved small town. I also realized that I'm *actually* more like the grumpy if (reluctantly) kind-hearted diner owner Luke, with his abhorrence of festivi-ties and celebration, his disdain for gifts ("What do I do with them?" he asks when Lorelai brings him Thanksgiving flow-ers, and she replies, "Ugh, not this again"), his classic flannel shirt and backwards baseball cap. The way he's generous with people he likes, but also not afraid to lash out when someone—say, Lorelai!—goes too far. He adores her, but he doesn't take her crap, or anyone's—except, briefly, Jess's, the wayward teenage nephew Luke does his best to surrogate-father. But eventually he gets tough with Jess, too. And otherwise, he chases down—sometimes literally, running out of the diner—any loser who messes with him.

Even when I'm on my fifth episode of the night and virtually snoring on the couch, as soon as he appears on-screen, I snap awake and tune in. I *get* Luke. He's the kind of person I like to think I am at my best—notwithstanding that he's a fictional diner owner in small-town Connecticut who spends his days serving coffee to townies, and I'm a real-life writer who sits alone in pajamas at a laptop in Upper Manhattan, cars whiz-zing by, sirens screaming.

So: Confession time. I'm writing this essay only halfway into season 4 (plus a few random later samplings) of *Gilmore Girls*; I've seen a mere eighty-some episodes, put in a scant sixtyish hours so far—not even half of the massive oeuvre. But I fully plan to view the rest of them now, including the revival. I've read about what happens—I decided to stop caring about spoilers—and I know that people are not thrilled with where Rory's story line goes (my late-twenties niece: "When you're young, it's easy to root for the main characters, to just assume they're right in every situation. But now I can see that Rory is an entitled brat, and Lorelai is a narcissist"—LOL!), or with how the show ends, or with the final season, 7, after Sherman-Palladino's departure. And I can't wait to watch all of those and see if I agree. Or rather, I can wait, and I do. I watch much more sporadically these days, doling out episodes only when I really have time, but savoring them when I do.

What's more, I feel a part of the *Gilmore Girls* community now—both the Stars Hollow TV one, which I experience vicariously, of course (my favorite way), and the vast, fervent club of watchers of the show, which I discover everywhere. I've become fluent at finding ways to bring up *GG* in conversations that, if they produce fellow fans, I can actually participate in—unlike those about the shows of my childhood (haven't seen it—never watched it—nope! I say, when someone mentions *Gunsmoke* or *General Hospital*, *Three's Company* or *Little House on the Prairie*). I'm excited to see who Lorelai and Rory meet, and date, in the rest of the seasons, and who they end up with. And to take in the details: What new lamps will be in Lorelai's house? How will Rory have her hair? Will Luke be as hot as ever? (Yup!) What will the regal Miss Patty be wearing?

So has watching *Gilmore Girls* made me more "normal"?

To be honest, that probably depends who you ask. But maybe it was never about becoming more normal, but simply about growing an appreciation for a type of TV that's an effortless escape, not to mention a guaranteed laugh. I get now, maybe for the first time, how television can be a balm, a salve . . . not unlike a certain kind of novel, I guess, but without even having to imagine the characters or the setting, let alone hold up your arms or turn pages. Because they're all in living color, right there.

A few nights ago, my daughter appeared at my apartment seeking consolation from a bad day. TV was never that in our relationship; we would always just talk, or I might suggest a book or two for distraction. But that night, she said, "Maybe we could just watch *Sex and the City*?" "Okay," I said (having of course never seen it), and then, "But after that, can I play you this episode of *Gilmore Girls* that I think you'll really love?" Her mouth opened. "Are you serious?" she said. "What has *happened* to you?"

Gilmore Girls happened. And I'm all in.

In Defense of Rory Gilmore

Annabelle Mei

Lorelai and Rory Gilmore are one of the most iconic mother-daughter duos in television history. The two are introduced in the pilot "more like friends than mother and daughter," with Rory picking up many habits from her mother. Throughout the seasons, however, Lorelai remains lovable, while Rory's popularity with the audience plummets. This is mostly attributed to decisions she made that were disapproved of by viewers, and often Lorelai as well. I started watching *Gilmore Girls* with my mother shortly after my parents got divorced. We had just moved across town when my mom suggested we watch a show together. As we entered the world of Stars Hollow, we immediately recognized the similarity between our relationship and that of Lorelai and Rory.

A coffee-obsessed mother-daughter duo who told each other everything, stumbling their way through life and love. We happily watched and rewatched our favorite episodes until we memorized them.

I remember sitting down one day with a *Gilmore Girls*-related question and going to the internet only to make a shocking discovery. Along with articles ranking Rory's boyfriends, Rory reading lists, and #rorygilmoreoutfit videos (because apparently Rory has since become a fashion icon on TikTok) were dozens of articles about why Rory is the worst character in *Gilmore Girls*, Rory's worst moments, and why people can't stand Rory. There are compilations of clips of Rory messing up and videos explaining her downfall. I was shocked. I knew that Rory had made some questionable decisions, and while I did not agree with all of her actions and behaviors, the amount of hate was astonishing. Rory does not deserve the hate she gets, as all of her decisions can be traced back to previous choices, making them consistent and in character, as well as mirroring the behavior of those around her. This does not mean people have to agree with her decisions, but should be taken into consideration when looking at Rory's character and her arc throughout the series. *Gilmore Girls* is a circular show, meaning that the special released in 2016 brings our characters back to the beginning, with Rory in a similar position to Lorelai at the top of the show.

For the first few seasons, Rory is unproblematic. She's the smart kid and the good daughter. She has a nice boyfriend and gets good grades. She butts heads with Paris and Tristan, but no more than most high schoolers, and nothing worth vilifying her for in the eyes of the viewers. At the end of season 2, however, we get the first view of one of the biggest issues with Rory. In "I Can't Get Started" (episode 22), Rory and Lorelai are at Sookie and Jackson's wedding when Jess moves back to Stars Hollow. Throughout the first two seasons, Rory has been steadily dating Dean, but Jess's arrival in season 2 starts to cause issues. It is clear from their interactions that the two are attracted to each other, but Rory is unwilling to end things with Dean. After a walk with her father, Christopher, Rory encounters Jess, who tells her that he is moving back, and she impulsively kisses him. She immediately panics and tells him to forget about it before fleeing.

While definitely unfair to Dean, it is not out of character for Rory to act impulsively. Rory's emotions often lead her to make rash decisions. A single conversation with Dean almost convinces her to reject Chilton and stay at Stars Hollow High. Christopher has just put forth the idea of him and Lorelai getting back together. Rory's hopes for her mother's potential relationship, and her slowly falling out of love with Dean, lead her to kiss Jess. This is the first instance of infidelity from Rory throughout the seasons. The kiss confirms Jess's role as one of Rory's love interests, as well as setting up much of the conflict in the next season.

While Rory gets a lot of hate for her treatment of Dean when Jess arrives, this being the first major strike, it is important to realize that Lorelai herself is attending the wedding with Christopher, her ex-boyfriend and Rory's father. Despite their close relationship, Christopher is actually dating Sherry Tinsdale at the time, having not broken off their relationship, though he tells Lorelai that he is planning on breaking up with her. One of the major reasons to overlook Lorelai's infidelity while bringing attention to Rory's is the fact that Rory's relationship status is one of the main story lines, while Lorelai and Christopher are portrayed as star-crossed lovers, with it never being the right time. Viewers are torn as to whether Rory should be with Jess or Dean, while Christopher and Sherry's relationship has been deteriorating, and we would prefer him to end up with Lorelai.

Unfortunately, Rory having an affair is something that returns twice, first in season 4 and again in the special *Gilmore Girls: A Year in the Life*. In the season 4 finale, "Raincoats and Recipes" (episode 22), Rory and Jess have broken up and Dean is married to Lindsay. Lorelai, Sookie, and Michel have finally opened their own inn, the Dragonfly Inn, and are having a test run with friends and family before their official opening. At some point Lorelai asks Rory to go home and get some CDs so guests can listen to music. While there, Dean shows up and expresses dissatisfaction with his marriage to Lindsay, telling Rory, "It's over. We both feel it." The two make their way to Rory's bedroom and they sleep together.

The parallels between mother and daughter are extremely common in this show. It is often pointed out how similar the two are. Immediately after being caught, Rory has the following conversation with Lorelai:

LORELAI: I didn't raise you to be like this. I didn't raise you to
be the kind of girl who sleeps with someone else's husband.
RORY: You slept with Dad when he was with Sherry.
LORELAI: He wasn't married to Sherry.
RORY: He was engaged, and she was pregnant.
LORELAI: So this is all my fault? I set one crappy example for
you, and you have no choice but to follow in my footsteps?

While cheating on Rory's part is definitely wrong, it is acknowledged in the story by the characters. It was previously established as something Rory does, as well as potentially being one of the many learned behaviors Rory got from her mother. When looking at this event, there are a few major things to consider, the first of which being Dean's role in the affair. Dean is the one who shows up to the Gilmore house with the intention of sleeping with Rory despite being married. Rory immediately brings up his marriage to Lindsay, which he quickly dismisses. Dean admittedly got married very young, not long after breaking up with Rory. He is clearly hung up on Rory, having fought with Jess over her through the entire past season. Rory's familiarity and comfortability with Dean causes her to start a friendship with him, but he continuously pursues a romantic relationship before ultimately destroying his own marriage.

In addition to Dean's role in the affair, this major event in

Rory's romantic life coincides with both Lorelai's relationship with Luke and Emily's marriage with Richard. While it is not uncommon for many story lines to come to a boiling point during the season finale, this is not the first time the Gilmore women's love lives have coincided. In season 2, for instance, Christopher's return matches Jess's return. "Raincoats and Recipes" has each woman in a parallel scenario. Emily and Richard's marriage is tested this season, with the two being separated at this time.

This comes to a head when they get stuck together at the Dragonfly Inn by their daughter and see Jason Stiles, Lorelai's ex-boyfriend and Richard's former business associate, there. They blow up at Lorelai and storm out. Rory and Dean sleep together, which deals a massive hit to how Rory is received; and after two narrative failures, Luke finally confesses to Lorelai and the two kiss. This event is very important for both Rory and Dean. It offers Dean a fresh start without Lindsay, and after the two break up, Rory is finally able to move on from Dean.

The second thing that upsets *Gilmore Girls* fans is that at the end of season 5, Rory decides to drop out of Yale. Rory has been pursuing a career in journalism, and has just finished an internship at the *Stamford Eagle Gazette*, the newspaper owned by the father of her boyfriend, Logan Huntzberger. In the penultimate episode of season 5, "Blame Booze and Melville" (episode 21), Logan's father, Mitchum Huntzberger, tells Rory that she isn't cut out to be a journalist and she is crushed. She flees to Logan and the two impulsively steal a yacht. While steal-

hello, cornstarch!

ing has never been something Rory has done, acting impulsively under stress is definitely in character. Yacht theft aside,
once Lorelai bails her out, Rory explains what happened and,
shockingly, Lorelai expresses understanding and their relationship remains relatively intact.

It is only in "A House Is Not a Home" (season 5, episode
22), when Rory tells Lorelai that she's not going back to Yale
the next year, that Lorelai gets upset. Lorelai warns Rory that
leaving Yale will cause her to lose momentum. Rory responds
with, "All I've been doing is working toward being a journalist! I'm not going to be a journalist, so what momentum am I
losing, exactly?" Rory has been working toward this since the
beginning of the show, with Paris revealing her intention to
become a journalism major back in "The Lorelais' First Day at
Chilton" (season 1, episode 2). Rory has just reached a major
hurdle and, with Mitchum Huntzberger's discouragement,
she decides to take a step back.

While dropping out of college seems totally out of left field,
the reason is actually much simpler than "bad writing" or acting without thinking: Rory Gilmore is burnt out. Since the
pilot, Rory has been the smart kid, she has always been working toward something. At first it is getting into Harvard, then
it's getting hired at the *Yale Daily News*, then it's getting an
actual journalism job. Rory has been chasing an ever-distant
finish line, one that at this point has been completely derailed
by Mitchum Huntzberger. Rather than relentlessly throwing
herself at a lofty goal, she steps back to decide whether journalism is something she wants to pursue despite this.

After spending a few weeks with her grandparents' rich lifestyle, she ultimately decides that, yes, she does want to pursue journalism. Rory's break from college also gives the viewers some new context about the lifestyle of Emily and Richard, as well as some of what Lorelai's life could have been like had she not gotten pregnant with Rory. Unsurprisingly, it is extremely privileged. While at first she seems content, Jess returns in "Let Me Hear Your Balalaikas Ringing Out" (season 6, episode 8) to find Rory with Logan, and finds the girl he once dated is almost gone. He says something that almost all of the viewers had been thinking for the past few episodes: "This isn't you. [. . .] What are you doing? Living at your grandparents' place, being in the DAR, no Yale . . . Why did you drop out of Yale?!" Jess's encouragement pushes Rory to reconnect with her mother, move out of Emily and Richard's house, and return to Yale with a plan to graduate on time.

Nowadays, people have a tendency to work themselves to death. Rory taking a break is something not often seen on television. Usually when one is faced with adversity, the message is try harder. While potentially frustrating to watch, characters—and people—are allowed to mess up, make mistakes, and get thrown off course. Life doesn't always turn out the way we expect, especially for the Gilmores. There is a double standard in *Gilmore Girls* that everyone can mess up . . . except Rory. She is described in the show as being an overachiever, which often eclipses the fact that she is far from perfect. *Gilmore Girls* follows Lorelai and Rory for seven years, and expecting to watch a teenager grow into a young adult without blundering a few times is unrealistic. Rory is expected to do better than Lorelai, who herself has done amazing things, including building an incredible life for her and Rory essentially with no support.

Once in a position to help Rory, Lorelai desperately wants Rory to do better, to the point where she is willing to force Rory to go to Chilton, saying that Rory will "get to do all the things that [she] never got to do." Rory is burdened with expectations that at times overwhelm her.

A final thing to consider is the show's ending. While Amy Sherman-Palladino left the writers' team when her contract wasn't renewed for the final season, she knew what she wanted the last four words of the show to be. In the final episode of *Gilmore Girls: A Year in the Life*, Rory reveals to her mother that she is pregnant. Obviously, Rory is not sixteen, and Lorelai will certainly not act like her mother, but this brings the show full circle, with Rory in Lorelai's shoes. While some have interpreted it as hinting at the potential of a spin-off, it is really unnecessary. We have already seen how the Gilmores handle situations like this.

By the end of the series, Lorelai has finished the story that Rory's final words begin to tell. We have known these characters for over a decade; the things that will play out will not be surprising. Rory's story, failures and all, is very human. She starts the show as a teenager full of potential and expectations. Over the course of seven seasons, we see her stumble her way through life, ending up as a young adult who is unsure of what to do next. It can be hard to live up to expectations, self-imposed or otherwise. Rory's struggles with her future are something that so many young people nowadays, including myself, can relate to. There are so many possibilities, but everything can feel just out of reach.

The characters in *Gilmore Girls* are fascinating; with so much content, they stay shockingly consistent. They are popular because people can recognize them in people they know. Every grumpy, lovable coworker is a Michel. Every crazy best friend is a Lane or a Paris. Every old friend who can set you back on track is a Jess. Every old lover who never gets the timing right is a Christopher. Every coffee-obsessed mother-daughter is Lorelai and Rory Gilmore. Despite her mistakes, I still relate to Rory a lot. *Gilmore Girls* will always be one of my favorite shows. Lorelai and Rory still remind me of me and my mother.

The Incredible Bookishness of Being a Gilmore

Tracey Minkin

S he had me at *Moby-Dick*.

While it took me fourteen years to discover *Gilmore Girls*, it only took eighteen minutes into the pilot episode to discover a girl reading *Moby-Dick* for fun, who'd read *Madame Bovary* the week before that—also for fun. A girl who hauled books around with her, who read them on park benches, read them standing in line, read them on buses and at the breakfast table. A girl who read *everywhere*. A girl whose bedroom was like an overstuffed little library (books shoved onto shelves, under the bed, and in her dresser drawers). A girl whose backpack groaned not only with her schoolbooks, but usually with four more volumes—a novel (Faulkner), a biography (Edna St.

Vincent Millay), a collection of essays (Vidal), and another of short stories (Welty). A girl who jumped off the sofa to see her grandfather's copy of Mencken's *Chrestomathy*, who gave her first boyfriend *The Metamorphosis* for Christmas. A girl who went to her winter formal with *The Portable Dorothy Parker* shoved into her evening bag.

At minute 18:25, I had yet to learn all this about Rory Gilmore. That lay ahead in the seven original seasons of the most book-filled TV series of all time (more on that later). But what I saw in that first episode—and what bonded me to Rory so quickly—was that here was a teen voluntarily—avidly—reading above her weight. Rory Gilmore not only read voraciously. She read audaciously.

Despite being deeply into middle age while watching *Gilmore Girls* in 2014 on Netflix, what I recognized was a girl like me. A *Moby-Dick* reader. A bookworm.

I was that kid, and other bookworms no doubt also saw themselves in Rory. We all displayed early that thirst for reading, with little thought to the setting or what we read. Newspapers, sure, but also every listing in *TV Guide*. Tiny ads in the backs of magazines. The arcane minutiae on cereal boxes, the outsize exhortations of billboards. And books, books, books. On the rare occasions my parents included kids in dinner out at a restaurant, even one fancy enough to serve Shirley Temples, they let me bring a book and read it on my lap until the food arrived—this began with a *Peanuts* collection when I was four. On my first day of school in 1966, I walked into kindergarten and wandered toward the bulletin board: Leaves of orange, green, and brown construction paper were stapled in a breezy cascade. Five words—spelled out with precut, shiny letters in a jolly fat typeface—ribboned across the top.

"Leaves fall in the autumn," I read out loud.

The next morning, I walked into first grade. An official grade-skipper, I was now the youngest kid in the room, but I might also have been the proudest. Reading had propelled me forward. Reading was not only my habit, it had suddenly become my badge of honor. For the rest of my youth and into adulthood, it was something I nursed—maybe even wielded—as self-definition. I didn't just read. I was a *reader*.

What is it that turns young readers from voracious to audacious? Maybe it's happenstance, or even stance itself. While still in elementary school, I discovered an easily accessible bottom shelf in my public library with a murderers' row—literally—of the works of Edgar Allan Poe. The librarian let me check these books out without any kind of parental permission (like many kids then, I walked for blocks, alone, to do things like go to the library, alone). But there's no *You Must Be This Tall to Ride* sign at a librarian's desk. You want to read Poe? Here's your Poe. Just don't forget to return it on time.

One summer not long ago, I drove over to Woodstock, New York, from my home in the Hudson Valley to see the author Neil Gaiman receive an award from the town library as part of its annual book fair. As part of his thanks, he told a story about his English, working-class parents needing child care during summer months and dropping him off, age eight, at the local library every morning. There, he said, librarians helped him work his way through the children's card catalog and into the adult one, suggesting books, treating him as a fellow reader. I teared up. "Protect your libraries," he cautioned the crowd. I cheered, weepily.

Are librarians the original enablers of book-mad children? Is it the elementary school teacher who presses advanced books into the hands of a precocious reader who's roared through every slender, age-appropriate thing at the back of the classroom? Is bookishness inspired or inherited? We don't know for sure about Rory Gilmore: we meet her as a high school sophomore reading *Moby-Dick* for fun. We get some biographical tuck-ins along the way: she's read, by her own count, about three hundred books so far (murmured in trilled despair while visiting Harvard and regarding its collection of thirteen million volumes—how will she read them all if this is her rate?). She read Ayn Rand's *The Fountainhead* at age ten but confesses to Jess Mariano that she made no sense of it so read it again at fifteen. Here is a kid who made her mother have her twelfth birthday party at the Mark Twain House & Museum (a real and wonderful place in Hartford, Connecticut)—what more evidence do we need of Rory's deep and long-standing bookishness?

And where did this all come from?

For me, it was my father, a family doctor who spent his days off sprawled in our den reading books. My mother was a magazine-leafer; ironically, I ended up becoming a magazine editor, but I tied my reading boat early to my father's. Like a sporting dad would take an athletic kid to the park to shoot free throws on the weekend, my dad took me on Saturdays to one of our small town's several bookstores—this one cheekily named Fahrenheit 451—where I twirled the spindly metal paperback stands to pick out a book he would then buy for me. This was middle-class indulgence, a privilege to be sure, and even then I felt like the luckiest tween ever. I'd blown through an early Ray Bradbury completist phase, flamed out on science fiction when it got too technical, marched through a stack of Steinbeck, and felt ready for bigger books, harder books. In seventh grade, I discovered a plastic box of index cards kept by our school librarian (librarians again!) at the checkout counter—a *Borrowers*-size collection of handwritten summaries from other bookish middle schoolers. I went here for ideas as a precocious seventh grader, searching for book advice like other girls my age scanned *Seventeen* for tips on outfits and makeup. I read a report, or so I thought, on a book called *Narcissus and Goldmund*. It was, I read, squinting at some fellow preteen's scrawl, about a pair of moths.

Of moths? Amazing! Hermann Hesse, I told my dad. This weekend I want to buy this book.

My father, who later lapsed into stealthily advancing dementia by his early sixties, died unmoored from the hundreds of books he'd devoured, from his medical knowledge, from everything eventually, before I could think to ask him what he must have thought of his ridiculously (not to mention misinformed) audacious reader. But he bought me the Bantam paperback—no moths on the cover should have been a tell—for $3.50, and I dug in.

And dug and dug. Oh. *Monks*. Okay. Not so alluring, even for a bookworm. But I finished it not so much out of literary thirst as because what else would I do? Much like Rory soldiered through her Ayn Rand at age ten, I struggled through Hesse at age eleven. I didn't get it, I didn't love it, but like a mountaineer who acclimates to thinner air over time, I refused to give up the altitude of big, adult books.

I am reminded of the wonderfully unsentimental confession in *To Kill a Mockingbird*, when Scout, another bookish protagonist, tells us: "Until I feared I would lose it, I never loved to read," she says. "One does not love breathing."

The bookish read as we breathe. It's part of our autonomic nervous system. To not read is unimaginable. And young bookworms like Scout Finch, Rory Gilmore, all of us, rarely if ever give up on a book. That's a habit acquired by aging readers (now me) who feel death nearing and can't waste time reading things we fear—or have enough discretion to decide—are not worth reading. There's a time for youthful omnivorous indiscrimination, not unlike the now-anachronistic practice of reading the dictionary—something bookish kids did when they were either bored or suddenly aspirational, or just poking around after looking something up. There's nothing more profoundly indiscriminate than alphabetical order. To follow that line through language is a guarantee of discovery.

What led Rory Gilmore to reach for Ayn Rand at ten? There's barely a mention of a library in Stars Hollow; to my thinking, a rare overlook by the team stitching together the cultural needlepoint of its fictional New England town. There's a bookstore, and in season 5, Rory snags a temporary job there over college spring break, sorting and inventorying books. For me the viewer, and for every bookworm watching *Gilmore Girls*, it's a dream most of us never realized—to be paid to spend every day among books. (Rory speaks for us all, in episode 16, when she agrees with Lane—sitting next to a tower of eighteen books she has already set aside to buy—that this job is costing her a fortune.)

What about her mother? Lorelai may have dropped out of high school at sixteen to have Rory, but she's got plenty of bookish name-checks amid the pop-culture barrage that so defined the character—and the show. In fact, the very first literary reference in *Gilmore Girls*—barely a minute and a half into the entire series—belongs to Lorelai, who puts a guy hitting on her in his place when he tells her he's on his way to Hartford, Connecticut. "You're a regular Jack Kerouac," she purrs.

And what of Richard Gilmore, the series' paterfamilias? Rory's grandfather is a big reader with tastes that run, not unpredictably, to Greatest Generation canonical—*History of the Peloponnesian War*, Euclid's *The Elements*, Shakespeare, and all six volumes of *The History of the Decline and Fall of the Roman Empire*, which takes him decades to finally finish, he confesses to his granddaughter, after asking what she's reading (P. G. Wodehouse). He purchases a hundred-year-old leather-bound copy of *Leaves of Grass* as a gift for Rory that he finds on a European trip. It's in Greek. There's no context, but Rory is thrilled. Richard Gilmore contains, we are left to imagine, multitudes.

The world of Stars Hollow, in fact, contains multitudes

when it comes to bookishness. With three generations of Gilmores reading books—Rory Gilmore the supernova CNN of reading—all books, all the time—and with everyone talking, all the time, and fast, all the time, *Gilmore Girls* characters hold books, read books, talk about books, refer near-constantly to books and authors. It's a cultural soundtrack, and TV has seen nothing like it, before or since. But like a soundtrack, it can wash over you quickly . . . unless you happen to have the DVDs, can hit pause, and start counting it all up.

Which is what an Australian *Gilmore* fan and writer named Patrick Lenton did. In 2013, a year before Netflix would bring the series back in its entirety and supercharge an entire new wave of fans, Lenton published on a literary blog in Australia a painstakingly compiled list of every book referenced on the series: an astonishing 339 books (it's daunting to read just the list in one pass). And while that close read of the series could be marked as achievement enough, Lenton doubled down: he vowed to read every book on the list. He dubbed it the "Rory Gilmore Reading Challenge."

What a thing! For readers, this is like having your statue erected in marble in the town square. A reading list—a reading *challenge*—in your name. Rory Gilmore was vaulted from TV teen to capital-R-capital-G titular cultural touchstone. Working through his list in alphabetical order (rather than chronological, by appearance on the show), Lenton was on book number eighteen, *Balzac and the Little Chinese Seamstress* by Dai Sijie, when a BuzzFeed reporter caught up to him in the spring of 2014. And when a BuzzFeed reporter publishes a list—

any list—it's only a matter of time before all of America surges into the moment. Just months before Netflix announced that it would be releasing the entire *Gilmore Girls* oeuvre into its binge-a-verse, readers of all kinds found a new flame to flutter around. The effect was titanic—a celebration of this bookish show, a celebration of its bookish protagonist, and an inherent challenge that drew hard-core *Gilmore* fans and book lovers who may never have even watched the show into one wonderful, virtual book club. It was phenomenon time.

That phenomenon has only deepened and broadened in the intervening decade. Once I started poking around online, I fell into a happy parallel universe of *Gilmore* book lists, challenges, bloggers, and even a robust Rory Gilmore Book Club that posts prompts and offers a custom spreadsheet to keep track of your reads. On Goodreads, a community of thousands pops in and out to discuss the list, discuss the show, and hypothesize what Rory would be reading today. Here you find nonreaders inspired to read audaciously after watching the show, you find veteran readers enjoying the game of it all. The internet, despite its best intention to trample the old-fashioned thrill of a book, seems here to be keeping the ideal aloft.

But I knew nothing about any of this when I discovered *Gilmore Girls*. I missed the BuzzFeed article back in 2014 and only started watching because Netflix recommended it to me, no doubt an algorithmic response to my deep replay history of *Friends* and dalliance with *Friday Night Lights*. As I piled up the episodes night after night, I nodded in love and nostalgia for a girlhood spent among books. But I noticed a keen difference between Rory and me. My books kept boys away. Hers attracted them.

Maybe it had nothing to do with the books themselves, but more with the fact that I look nothing like the colt-like, symmetrically marvelous Alexis Bledel, who, I learned, was scooped straight from a young modeling career into the show. (She was so unaccustomed to acting that Lauren Graham often held her by the shoulders in early episodes—this was not affection-acting; it was helping Bledel hit her camera marks. Graham, on the other hand, became series creator Amy Sherman-Palladino's top pick for the role because she could pronounce "Kerouac" on cold reading.)

But Alexis Bledel set aside, I wonder: Does loving books forestall loving boys? Or more specifically, does audacious reading—choosing *Moby-Dick* as a symbol of aspiring intellect—ward off the capitulation of sexuality? Does bookishness both signal and defend virginity? Are those other bookish heroines—Elizabeth Bennet, Jo March, Hermione Granger, Matilda, even an animated Belle—all the purer for their devotion to reading? Until, eventually, they fall in love and all the books seem to fly out the window. Or remain shelved in the library.

Bookishness *drew* boys to Rory Gilmore. Her first boyfriend—Dean—spies her reading and is smitten with a girl who could concentrate that hard while a flag football game broke into a fight behind her. "I thought, 'I've never seen anyone read so intensely before in my entire life. I have to meet that girl,'" he says to her, then confesses that she's also nice to look at. That's a creepy pickup line at any age, but it also teaches that for a bookworm to be attractive, she needs to look more like Alexis Bledel and less like me.

Beauty aside, in the *Gilmore* universe, books are central to Rory's allure. She gets Dean with them. She certainly gets Jess with them (and he gets her, swiping her copy of *Howl* right out of her bedroom to mark it up with notes in the margins). It's scary, in a way, to witness these young men romance Rory by invading her space—Dean stalks her, Jess marks up her book. It might get kicked out of the writers' room now, but in the aughts, invasion—if only via books, anyway—is romantic. A love language.

And for Rory, books are her language of seduction. When Dean finishes a Jane Austen novel Rory's pressed upon him, it's better than if he'd scored the winning touchdown under Friday Night Lights. They flirt over whether he liked it; he parries with admonishing her to read Hunter S. Thompson. After discovering Rory has brought him cookies, he asks how he can repay her, and she says he can read some Charlotte Brontë next. Sparks fly!

Rory's moody, more intellectual boyfriend number two, Jess Mariano, is Rory's ultimate book-talk-as-foreplay scene partner—they're never not tussling about books, tossing references at each other in a chaste striptease. Books are sexy in Rory's world. And, I suppose, the less Bledel-like rest of us eventually find partners who find our bookishness attractive, who enter our strange world—although sometimes it takes college, life, a sense of reality, to bring like minds together.

I found a bookish husband in 1982 and recall our nights spent, TV off, set in nearby chairs, reading. We often, in the days before Amazon, shopped for books on weekends, a coda to my father's and my rhythm. We kept a version of my middle school librarian's book report file, only ours was a blank-paged book. Book reports! In our thirties!

In my case, as well as Rory's, the most bookish of pairings don't always last. We fall out of love, we blunder, we get divorced, we fall in love again, but we keep reading. I can't guarantee Rory Gilmore's future—the 2016 capsule series gave us a peek, but I think we all agree it was better imagining her trajectory than inhabiting it. Having swum in the bookish waters of *Gilmore Girls* and discovered the passionate world of Rory Gilmore-inspired book club members, TikTokers, and Instagrammers, to witness a world of modern women (and men) reading with attack, with audacity, is a deeply comforting legacy. To have an early-aughts TV show with its crazily bookish joie de vivre light up my laptop and remind me of how much reading has been a part of my life, how time is running out against the Harvard thirteen million, and how I'd best put some things down and pick up a book.

Digger and Me

Michael Ruhlman

Early in 2017, I moved in with Lorelai and Rory Gilmore, although I didn't know it. I didn't know the show *Gilmore Girls*. I'd never heard of the land called Stars Hollow. By name my Lorelai and Rory happened to be Ann Hood, novelist and editor of this collection, and her daughter Annabelle. They'd been living in a loft in Providence, just the two of them, for the better part of a year when I moved in.

Needless to say, with Ann's and my marriage in the offing, I wanted to fit into the girls' routine, which I was fundamentally changing. They were fiercely attached to one another. And the intensity of their bond was something that excluded me. I wanted Annabelle, thirteen at the time, to like me, of course.

I tried to do what I could, making her stovetop popcorn with butter, serving her a poached egg on toast in bed.

But mostly I annoyed her. I left cupboards open. I used a mug for an afternoon cup of tea that read *You're the Rory to my Lorelai*.

"Ruhlman!" She called me Ruhlman for that entire first year. "How dare you?" She wasn't kidding. This was a sacred mug.

I'd pick a different mug next time, nothing with any hint of *Gilmore Girls*. I chose one that read *Oh, I can't stop drinking the coffee . . . I stop drinking coffee, I stop doing the standing & walking & the words-putting-into-sentence doing*.

"Ruhlman!"

Remind me again, Ann, why does this Christmas ornament say *I smell snow*?

Annabelle, who was roughly Rory's age when she began watching, and Ann were *Gilmore Girls* fanatics. And I was glad for them, mother and daughter sharing something so deeply pleasurable, a beautifully written series about a mother and her teenage daughter. But it was also something I was excluded from. And no one likes to be excluded, even if what you're being excluded from isn't something you really want to do anyway. At least no one with the not-uncommon genetic disorder known as FOMO, such as myself.

By the following summer, they were well into season 4. Annabelle had just finished her sophomore year of high school and Ann had an afternoon free. What they did, of course, was carry on to the next episode of *Gilmore Girls*.

We lived in a big sunny loft in which the living room, dining room, and kitchen were all one. At the time I typically worked at the dining room table, with a view of the backs of two heads watching *Gilmore Girls*.

I normally wouldn't have paid attention, but on this day in June, I heard a familiar voice and looked up. I said, "Chris Eigeman is on this show?"

Both gasped and turned to me.

Annabelle said, "You know Digger?"

"I do," I said, happy to share in even this smidge of *Gilmore Girls* fandom.

I'd seen *Metropolitan*, the first in a trilogy of films by Whit Stillman, in 1990. This was Chris Eigeman's first movie and he basically steals the show as Nick Smith, a sardonic, deadpan Upper East Side socialite who gives snobbism and the bourgeoisie a good name. For Smith, being a debutant or a debutant escort is about more than coming out into society, it's part of the moral clarity and code of ethics bound up in how to live well.

I still love this movie. I and my friends eagerly went to see the next two films by Stillman featuring many of the same characters, including the one played by Chris. Two decades later, I spotted a comment on my blog or on Twitter praising some offset spoons I'd made. (I used to have a small business manufacturing unique kitchen tools.) The commenter was one Chris Eigeman.

Could it be? One of my favorite comic actors in one of my favorite movies commenting on something I'd made?

I emailed him. It was indeed the one and only. He loved my spoons. I posted about a method for cooking a holiday goose. I believe he tried it and loved it. A distant friendship had begun thanks to social media, something that hadn't existed when Chris played Jason "Digger" Stiles in *Gilmore Girls* in 2003.

In 2012, married with children and living in Cleveland, I purchased a studio apartment in New York City, where I often had work. On one of my trips there, in 2013 or 2014, I asked if Chris could have dinner. We met at Barbuto, then across the street from my apartment. It was a splendid meal and conversation.

A little more than a year after that, in the fall of 2015, I found myself separated from my wife and living alone in that same West Village apartment. I'd spent virtually my entire life in Cleveland and had only one or two friends in New York. I was lonely and miserable. One activity that has always kept anxiety at bay has been playing pool. And I knew from our brief correspondence that Chris, likewise, loved to play pool. He'd even written and directed a film whose protagonist, a divorced, rough-around-the-edges young mom, earns money shooting pool (*Turn the River*, 2007).

I emailed Chris deep into that dark fall, told him of my new circumstances, and asked if we could meet to play pool. He suggested Amsterdam Billiards in the East Village. Over several games and several beers, I poured my heart out. He listened, commented in his wry, smart way, and generally did what he could to comfort and reassure me that all would be

well one day. I emailed him to thank him, expressing the sadness of my first holiday season alone.

"I absolutely wish you luck and hang in there," he wrote
back. "I have to believe the first of everything is the hardest—
first Thanksgiving, first Christmas . . . and then it gets easier
and better. See you soon." He added, "Just bought a holiday
passel of offset spoons and paddles. A gift you can always be
proud of. Safe travels, C."

Which is why, three years later, engaged to the editor of
this collection, I looked up when I heard Chris in conversation
with Lauren Graham, Jason Stiles to Graham's Lorelai.

After Annabelle and Ann both asked, "You know Digger?" I
sent a brief email to Chris—"You were on the *Gilmore Girls*?!"—
including a picture of the back of two heads watching Chris on
the screen. If he wrote back, this would give me some serious
cred with my about-to-be stepdaughter. I could, for a moment
anyway, join in their *Gilmore Girls* devotion.

Twenty minutes later an email from Chris appeared in my
inbox: "Oh yes," he wrote. "On it for a year. Really just keeping the bed warm till Luke gets there. Made a movie for Netflix
called *Seven in Heaven* they may enjoy. It's PG-13. Work well and
see you in the fall."

Proud of my insider information, I called out to Ann and
Annabelle a line I didn't understand but figured would be
self-explanatory to them. "He says he's just keeping the bed
warm for Luke."

"RUHLMAN!"

I had, of course, just spoiled a major, major plot point that would conclude season 4, namely that Luke and Lorelai, as everyone hoped, would ultimately be united in love. Annabelle was rightly pissed.

Over the next four years, one in pandemic isolation, Ann and Annabelle watched every *Gilmore Girls* episode of every season, all 153 of them, as well as the four movie-length episodes that make up *A Year in the Life*, a follow-up miniseries actually filmed nine years after season 7 concluded.

In all those years, I believe I watched two episodes with Ann and Annabelle, the very first two. And that was that. I let them have their *Gilmore Girls*. When I was on the road, they would have dinner and watch episodes of *Gilmore Girls*. I always called to say good night to Ann when we were apart, and my calls at ten or ten-thirty were typically returned via a text from Ann: "Watching another episode. Will call when we're done?"

Our time of COVID isolation ended and the world returned to its post-pandemic self.

Annabelle graduated high school and began college at Sarah Lawrence, near enough that Ann (we were now living permanently in my tiny West Village apartment) could drive up to Bronxville once a week to have lunch with her Rory.

Being in the city, I could coax Chris to one of my favorite bars, the Long Island Bar, which was right around the corner from where he lived with his wife and teenage son, so that Ann could meet Digger. And when this book began to come together, I all but begged Ann to write an essay about the actor I so admired and who had been so helpful to me when I was at a low point in my life. I actually had no idea that I would ultimately be writing about Ann and Annabelle, a facsimile of Lorelai and Rory—I simply said, I can get a behind-the-scenes look from one of the show's actors, I can get first-hand accounts of why one cast member thinks this show is so universally adored.

Ann gave in.

This assignment, of course, meant watching not just a couple of episodes but the entire season 4, which turned out to be kind of a dream job.

Gilmore Girls was written primarily by the husband-wife team Amy Sherman-Palladino and Daniel Palladino. Its crackling dialogue is dense and funny. No one lacks for a snappy comeback. And the episodes are so dialogue-heavy their scripts tend to be longer than those for most shows of the same duration. But who exactly was this Digger fellow who had given me an inroad into the Annabelle-Ann universe?

Season 4 has many distinct plotlines: Rory's first year at Yale; Lorelai's building out the inn; Luke's ongoing relationship with his ex-wife Nicole and his nephew Jess; Jess's bad-boy relationship with Rory; and, of course, Lorelai's relationship with a former childhood acquaintance, Jason "Digger" Stiles.

Digger, who does not like to be called by his childhood nickname, is a smooth, suave man Lorelai's age, the son of Richard Gilmore's former business partner. After Richard's acrimonious split with Jason's father, he and Jason build a competing firm together, while Jason begins to woo Lorelai, who is at first resistant, but ultimately is won over by his quirks, his wit, and charm. (Quirk, a biggie: the first night Lorelai spends with Digger, he asks her to sleep in the guest room.)

The main issue between Jason and Lorelai is that Lorelai refuses to tell her parents she and Jason are dating, largely fearing her formidable mother, Emily Gilmore (Kelly Bishop), who doesn't like Jason. This plotline comes to an end when Jason's father threatens to sue Richard (Edward Herrmann plays Lorelai's father). Richard has no recourse but to cut a deal with Jason's father, stabbing Jason in the back. Jason threatens to sue Richard. That crosses a line Lorelai can't abide, and she ends their relationship.

In Digger's final episode of that season, he shows up at Lorelai's inn's opening, unbidden but determined to win her back. He won't take no for an answer. But no is her final answer. After four long seasons of audience-teasing flirtations, Luke and Lorelai embrace at last. And goodbye, Digger.

I met Chris at Henry Public, a cozy, quiet bar not far from where he lives in Brooklyn Heights, to talk about the enduring appeal of *Gilmore Girls* and better understand my wife and her daughter and the other fans who have racked up 500 million viewing hours, according to Netflix.

"I loved everything about *Gilmore Girls*," he said, casting back exactly twenty years as he sipped his Jameson whiskey. "I loved Lauren. I loved sitting around with Kelly Bishop and talking about *A Chorus Line*." Bishop originated a major role in that musical, Sheila, in 1975 and won a Tony Award for it. "People would come up to her with the original cast album, and hold it out to her like a Eucharist.

"I loved Ed Herrmann. I loved doing scenes with him . . . Until he stabbed me in the back." Chris still remembers reading this episode's script and thinking, "Oh nooo, seriously?"

Chris adores Amy and Dan and their writing. He called my attention to a joke that had passed me by, it was so lean and quick. The first time Digger and Lorelai are together, Lorelai recalls the time Digger tipped over their canoe at camp. He tells her that this made him famous in his cabin thanks to braless Lorelai and her wet T-shirt. And it was how she got her nickname: Umlaut.

"That's the best-written joke I've seen," Chris said. "That's a really good joke. The line is super clean." And it is also, in the nine-years-after miniseries, the final word Digger says to Lorelai. "They know how much I love that joke," he said with a smile.

Of course, he was grateful to be "invited to be on something that was so beloved," but it did have its downside. "Countless seventeen-year-old girls in airports don't like me," he said. He was the sole person preventing True Love from happening to Lorelai and Luke. He remembers sitting in the Ambassador Lounge in one airport or another, and a woman stopped before him and said, "Excuse me, but how long is your contract on *Gilmore Girls* for?"

Once, returning to his home city, Denver, Colorado, he was leaving the airport and there was a woman holding a sign that read *I love Stars Hollow*, the fictional town of the show. She was evidently meeting strangers, perhaps a *Gilmore Girls* get-together or fan club. Chris couldn't resist. He passed by her closely and said, "I love Stars Hollow, too." The woman screamed with surprise and delight.

I asked Chris why he thought the show remains so enduring. He said he didn't know, then said, "When life is tough, when somebody's sick, *Gilmore Girls* shows up. It's like a balm. It's comforting. It's embracive. At root, it's optimistic. It knows what it is. And it's funny."

When he said that, something clicked. Ann and Annabelle had begun watching *Gilmore Girls* when Annabelle and her mom were beginning a new, uncertain life. Annabelle had left her childhood home. Ann was fiercely protective of her daughter, but she too had to navigate a whole new future, eating dinner off packing boxes in a loft in an unfamiliar neighborhood. But they had each other. And they had the comfort, embrace, humor, and optimism of *Gilmore Girls* when the day was done.

I watched the entirety of season 4, not just the thirteen episodes featuring Chris, up through Rory's losing her virginity and Lorelai and Luke's long-awaited embrace. What happened to me, of course, will be familiar to millions of viewers. I fell in love with *Gilmore Girls*, the great writing, the oddball recurring characters like Kirk, the almost Seinfeldian humor regarding life's minutiae, the extraordinary mother-daughter team of Lorelai and Rory, and, yes, as Chris had noted, its ultimate optimism and the feeling of comfort the show gives you, of living in their Stars Hollow world.

The other night, during Annabelle's winter break from Sarah Lawrence College (she's now a sophomore), as we were readying dinner and unable to decide what to watch, Ann said, "How about an episode of *Gilmore Girls*? I need to see 'Swan Song.'" Annabelle said, "I need to see 'The Prodigal Daughter Returns'!"

They turned to me. Would I roll my eyes? Quickly offer an alternative choice?

"I would love to watch *Gilmore Girls*," I said.

Ann said, "Finally."

Finally? It had never occurred to me that they'd want me to like the show over which they'd bonded during the entirety of Annabelle's teenage years. To be a part of this intense mother-daughter relationship. But they did. I love my wife like nothing else and we're deeply close. But now I truly felt a part of the two of them as I never had before.

Thanks, Digger.

Acknowledgments

Thank you to all the writers who contributed to this anthology and so beautifully told the world why *Gilmore Girls* endures. And thank you to Gail Hochman, who saw the potential in this right away. Thanks, too, to Jill Bialosky, who recognized my passion for *Gilmore Girls*, and to Erin Lovett and everyone at W. W. Norton who helps my ideas come to life. I'm grateful that Amy Sherman-Palladino created the show—maybe someday I can meet her and thank her in person—and grateful to everyone in it who kept me company when I needed comfort. Most of all, thank you to my darling daughter, who first introduced me to Lorelai and Rory and the world of *Gilmore Girls*, and to Michael, my very own Luke.

About the Contributors

YASSMIN ABDEL-MAGIED is the Sudanese-born author of five books, most recently *Stand Up and Speak Out Against Racism* (Candlewick, 2023). Previous titles include the essay collection *Talking About a Revolution* (Penguin Random House, 2022) and the award-winning teen novel *Listen, Layla* (Puffin, 2021).

ERIN ALMOND is the author of the novel *Witches' Dance*. Her essays and short fiction have appeared in the *Boston Globe*, the *Sun*, *Colorado Review*, *Pangyrus*, *Literary Mama*, and WBUR's Cognoscenti column. She is a graduate of the UC Irvine MFA program and can be found online at www.erineileenalmond.com.

RAND RICHARDS COOPER is the author of *The Last to Go* and *Big as Life*. His writing has appeared in *The New Yorker*, *Harper's*,

Esquire, *The Atlantic*, and *Best American Short Stories*. A longtime contributor to *Bon Appétit* and former restaurant critic for the *New York Times*, he lives in Hartford, Connecticut.

Born in Puerto Rico, ANJANETTE DELGADO writes about sexile, heartbreak, and social justice. She's the author of two award-winning novels and the editor of *Home in Florida: Latinx Writers and the Literature of Uprootedness* (University Press of Florida, 2021). Her work has appeared in the *New York Times*, *Prairie Schooner*, NPR, and elsewhere.

NINA DE GRAMONT is the author of nine books, most recently *The Christie Affair*, which was a Reese Witherspoon book club pick and a *New York Times* best seller, and has been translated into more than twenty languages. She teaches creative writing at the University of North Carolina Wilmington.

CATHI HANAUER is the *New York Times* best-selling author of three acclaimed novels and two essay anthologies, *The Bitch in the House* and *The Bitch Is Back* (an NPR Best Book of 2016). She's written for the *New York Times*, the *Washington Post*, *Elle*, *O*, and others. Find her at www.cathihanauer.com.

ANN HOOD is a best-selling novelist and memoirist whose books include *The Knitting Circle*, *The Obituary Writer*, *The Book That Matters Most*, *Fly Girl*, and *Comfort: A Journey Through Grief*, which was named one of the top ten nonfiction books of 2008 by *Entertainment Weekly*. She has also written middle-grade and

YA novels and *The Treasure*, a ten-book series for middle-grade readers. Her most recent book is the novel *The Stolen Child*.

ANNABELLE MEI is a queer theater-maker and artist based in New York City and Providence, Rhode Island. She loves coffee, cats, and traveling the world with her friends and family. Thank you, Mom, for being my Lorelai.

TRACEY MINKIN is an award-winning magazine editor and writer based in New York's Hudson Valley. Serving as the travel editor at *Coastal Living* magazine, she also writes on a broad range of topics for many national magazines and digital outlets and is a contributing author for Wildsam and Lonely Planet guidebooks.

KATIE MOULTON is the author of the memoir *Dead Dad Club: On Grief & Tom Petty* (Audible). A MacDowell fellow, her essays appear in *The Believer*, the *Oxford American*, *New England Review*, the *Sewanee Review*, and elsewhere. She teaches in the Johns Hopkins University Writing Seminars and the Newport MFA.

FREYA NORTH is one of the UK's best-loved authors. She has written sixteen novels, exploring the emotion and complexities of everyday relationships and families. A sense of place is central to her work, with British Columbia, Vermont, France, and the beautiful British landscape as characters in their own right.

JOANNA RAKOFF is the author of the best-selling memoir *My Salinger Year* and the novel *A Fortunate Age*.

MICHAEL RUHLMAN, a *New York Times* best-selling author and three-time James Beard Award winner, has written more than twenty-five books of nonfiction, fiction, memoir, and cookbooks, the latter both on his own and as a collaborator with Michelin-starred chefs. He lives in New York City with his wife, Ann Hood.

SANJENA SATHIAN is the author of the critically acclaimed novel *Gold Diggers*, which was named one of the 10 Best Books of 2021 by the *Washington Post* and an NPR, Electric Lit, and Amazon Best Book. Her second novel, *Goddess Complex*, is out from Penguin Press in March 2025.

FRANCESCO SEDITA is a writer and children's book publisher. He's created the Pathfinders Society graphic novel series, and picture books like *This Is the First Book I Will Read to You* and *Our Italian Christmas Eve*. And he produced *The Who Was? Show* on Netflix. He is currently at work on a novel. Find out more about him at www.francescosedita.com.